SUPERSTITIONS
A GUIDE TO HABITS, CUSTOMS AND BELIEFS

PETER WEST

GREEN MAGIC

Green Magic
Seed Factory
Aller
Langport
Somerset TA10 0QN
England

www.greenmagicpublishing.com

Designed and typeset by K.DESIGN
Winscombe, Somerset

ISBN 9781838132422

GREEN MAGIC

Contents

Introduction

Superstition holds a fascination for us all and throughout our lives, whether we admit it or not, at one time or another we all give way to some level of incredulity regarding the supernatural while many tend to give it a completely misdirected irreverence.

Throughout the years, most superstitions have been handed down by word of mouth. There is such a variety of different ideas on the original themes that today society has a marvellously fascinating array of conflicting beliefs and thoughts whereby we have given ourselves very little room for manoeuvre in our attempts to not bow to them. Today, we accept them for what they seem to be rather than for what they actually are.

Specifically, to be superstitious implies a form of credulity regarding the supernatural, an irrational fear of the unknown or mysterious; there is a widely held but unjustified idea of the effects of the nature of a thing.

It may also be said to be a practice, opinion or religion based on these beliefs. In Roman times, superstition reflected an act or an attitude of piety. Later, church leaders who wished to gain the ascendancy and more power for themselves cleverly spread the word that those who believed in such things were really perpetuating and enacting religious or semi-religious acts that were basically Pagan or corrupt in their origin.

Today, we realise many of these widely held and unjustified opinions are universal no matter what the creed, culture or race of the believer. It is only in the way we view how each particular tale is "interpreted" or "translated" do we find that the belief is tailored to the society in which the believer belongs.

Many of the beliefs, sayings and other practices that the majority of us pursue or perpetuate prove this point. What we may say in Scotland will be more or less the same and presented along similar lines in Cornwall, although the actual belief will appear to have changed in some way by the people concerned.

Essentially, there is no reason, no positive fact, no direct cause or effect and no real argument that can actually triumph over instinct when we come to discuss this rather vexed field of superstitious belief. The simplest of examples will help prove the point.

Suppose you are indoors and you stand behind a closed window at home as you watch your spouse water the garden. A normal everyday occurrence, especially in the spring or summer months that so many of us are likely to do. Suddenly, they observe you watching and quite deliberately but playfully direct the hose to the window and the stream of water hits the glass.

Instinctively, you will step back or even duck but at one and the same time you know the water cannot reach you. And even if it could, it would not hurt you anyway – after all, water is essential to life! Your action has demonstrated your instincts have triumphed over reason.

In a nutshell, it sums up the basis of almost all superstitious belief: instinct prevailing over reason.

Two principal areas of superstition characterise this concept. One is to pursue a certain course of action that could result in bad luck (?), while the other is to follow a specified action in the hope or belief that it will bring the desired result – good luck (?).

Fundamentally, certain logical or illogical positive or negative actions are claimed to theoretically produce positive or negative results. But why do such superstitions persist and come with us into our adulthood?

It is easy to see or understand children being wary of such matters but by the time we reach maturity we really should know better. Perhaps it is due mostly to our own ignorance of certain things that we allow these beliefs to still exert their effect.

One of the best myths of all is that science can explain everything, so we wait for that to happen. Unfortunately, the majority of us are going to have a very long wait indeed...

Few people therefore, whatever their station in life, can escape the clutches of superstitious belief. It is a fairly wide-spread knowledge that even some of our present-day heroes like the modern spacemen will take steps to avoid alleged lucky or unlucky colours or may refuse to take certain actions prior to, during or even after missions.

This certainly follows on from the great heroes of the past. First the land explorers came, then the traders. Sea-going merchants were followed by the sea-faring explorers. Just think of all the stories, romances and yarns that came with them, many distorted by time and the telling of them.

The origins of some of our most outlandish folklore can be traced easily to these times while others are impossible to hunt down. Some may only be guessed, others merely hinted at. A few seem to have their beginnings at certain points of great historical events.

LADDERS

For example, few people will walk under a ladder, while many go to quite extreme lengths to avoid passing beneath one. Perhaps almost as many worry about reaching through the rungs to retrieve a lost article. This is regarded as an action that has always been considered to be very unlucky indeed!

In ancient times, castles, even whole towns were built like fortresses. The only way in would be by a drawbridge or a rope-lift of some kind to limit access to just a few at a time. So, when invading armies besieged these castles and towns the only way to get into these structures would have been by climbing up ladders placed on the outside walls.

This would have been achieved among all manner of fighting going on both on the ground below all the way up the ladders and on the battlements at the top. Those who ventured up the ladders were very brave men under the orders from even braver (?) leaders behind them.

The defenders on the battlements would be raining down almost everything on the attackers that they could find – stones, arrows and even boiling oil and water! Thus, the worst place to be was under one of these ladders.

Probably more people lost their lives while under the ladder than from being on them at such times. These luckless people had not only to dodge the defenders' missiles they would have also had to avoid a collection of bodies and weaponry dropping on them from a great height as well.

This is, perhaps, one of the most reasonable and logical accounts of the origin of this belief. However, according to the country and the reason for the ladder's use, a number of other explanations may be found – all equally acceptable.

In much older times, the ladder leaning against a wall formed a triangle – an old representation of the universal symbol of life. With the advent of Christianity, this soon became the symbol of the Holy Trinity. Thus, to walk under the leaning ladder was not only to show disrespect it also implied you might have an affinity with the devil!

Some very old paintings depicting the Crucifixion show a ladder leaning against the Cross with Satan raging under it but powerless to do ill as he has been cheated by Christ dying to save humanity. Again, this is yet another reason why the area under the ladder is considered to be bad luck.

One very old term still used on the continent, "under the ladder", refers to bad luck and means the person concerned is doomed never to succeed in their ambitions. This has been linked with someone who has been hanged and where undertakers whose business it was to retrieve the dead had to enter the space to prepare the executed person for burial. This description is thought by some to come from their actions whereby they had to retrieve the remains from under the ladder or other type of gallows.

This could have been a bit messy at such times as some felons were not always just simply hanged. In many areas these people were first hanged, then cut down, tortured, hanged, drawn and then quartered. Work under the platform, or the ladder, would have been a bit fraught and most certainly not for the squeamish.

Some of the more unscrupulous characters did a roaring trade in either the clothing or possessions of the departed while some dealt in actual body parts in an "under-the-counter" trade, something severely frowned upon but largely ignored by the authorities of the time. This is the principal origin of the phrase "under-the-counter" for any trade or dealings that were not exactly legal.

The Dutch believe that to actually reach through into the triangle is extremely unlucky because you have invaded a space not meant for you. In medieval times, in some parts of Holland and northern Europe it was thought that anyone who did do this ought to be hanged if caught.

next meal might come. Day-to-day life was difficult, few could really be trusted, even the neighbours. Enemies abounded the moment you stepped outdoors.

Rogues and vagabonds were everywhere. Travel was kept to a minimum with journeys rarely undertaken alone. Roads were non-existent and the law, such as it was, almost hardly ever observed or imposed. Rough justice held sway more than anything.

Today, most people think of travel as a simple matter of fact. They put on their hat and coat, open the front door and just go. Few think that what they are about to do is of any importance. They go shopping, pay a visit to the library, meet a friend for a coffee or go to work. Just over 200 years ago such ideas were virtually non-existent. No self-respecting woman would even think of going out alone. In many cases, she was not allowed. Women ventured forth with a male escort because it was then the expected thing to do. Although there were shops of a kind they were not as we know them today.

The road to the centre of a village or town bore little resemblance to what we use today. At the very outside, it was a cart track or a well-worn footpath. People did not travel far in those days but when they did, it was kept to a minimum. Inns and hostelries were the centres of information, and that is where everybody headed.

Here there would be the few travellers who were there because of their trade or profession. What news there was would have been spread by word of mouth. When this information was passed on by the locals back in their own homes it would have been slightly distorted. There were a few publications but few and far between for the most part, but then few could write and even less read. Think of the game of Chinese Whispers and think of it being played for real in every household. What Sam the groom said to his family would have been spoken of differently by William the third footman or by James the old poacher.

When, later, and in many cases very much later, family members did meet up, their own interpretations would have been discussed according to what and how (or if) they were told. The traveller passed on what may well have borne little semblance to the original. And who is to know if that the traveller had got it right in the first place...?

The further back in time one travels, the more this myth-information was likely to have been how almost any news was passed on. This is just one reason why superstitious beliefs can and do differ so radically in just a matter of ten or twenty miles or so. Remember, in those days we had no telephones; no radio or television and, as such, news programmes were still a long way off. People didn't discuss things over the garden fence in quite the way they did a hundred years ago. Even less were able to read or write.

In each age and in whatever part of the world we look, in Britain or in Europe, Asia, the Middle East, even North or South America, they all had communication problems. As a result, their beliefs and superstitions have been derived in much the same way that we have received ours.

Through each of these ages and civilisations disease and poor health, probably through malnutrition, not only gave birth to superstition and belief regarding their origins, they also included the very people who were supposed to cure these ills. Doctors or their equivalent in those days were feared more than anything or anyone else.

The one comfort that everyone had was their religion irrespective of what it was. In this country there is no doubt that Paganism was first. The Druids followed on, and then came the first "established" church that rode roughshod over them only to create more divisions: the Catholics, Puritans and Protestants.

They all took what they could from each other and did their very best to turn such matters to their favour. The Christians thought the early Pagan beliefs were merely superstition. Early Protestants thought the use of the rosary was also a superstition. And as for what the Druids believed – no one would or seemed to take them seriously.

All these religious practices are still very much in evidence, in many cases changed out of all proportion and recognition. But they are still there. Without doubt, the widest source of most superstitious practices stems from the religious beliefs of all denominations. Whether a comfort or a fear, from very early times to the present day, all superstitions, their beliefs and practices still abound. And, perhaps, for a few, there may be a grain of truth in them.

The Calendar

DAYS AND DATES, FEAST DAYS, TRAVEL AND WEATHER

Everybody wishes everyone else a "Happy New Year" when the calendar shows that another new twelve month period is about to start. It is a popular custom the world over but this short period is also loaded with superstitions. Many are quite similar in their theme but they do differ slightly from country to country and, within some of the larger nations, from area to area.

Of course, much of this depends on when you feel the New Year actually starts, for there were many different religions, beliefs and technicalities regarding the calendar in general use today.

In England, the New Year used to start on March 21 but now it is January 1. The Chinese New Year begins with the second New Moon after the (European) winter solstice (when the Sun enters Capricorn) of the previous year. The Greeks used July 1 while at one stage during the French revolutionary period, the French New Year began on September 21.

The Moslem New Year begins on a different date every year because it is only 354 days long and does not conform to the accepted modern civil year of 365 days. The ancient Irish used to celebrate St Brigid's Feast Day for their New Year on February 1.

When the Jews were experiencing the 5759th year of their calendar, the Japanese were enjoying their almanac's 2659th year. The Hindus were celebrating 2057 VE of their time system and, at least up to 1918, the Russians were using a very old time system but they eventually brought it all into line with the rest of the world after their revolution.

There are many other time systems in use all over the world. Because of this, and the fact that many are so widely different, tracing the origins of many of the superstitions associated with the celebration of the New Year can be rather difficult.

"First-footing" probably originated in Scotland, perhaps even earlier if we bear in mind their Celtic history. This superstition demands that the first visitor after midnight has struck should be a dark-haired man carrying the simple gifts of a small value coin, a little lump of coal, or wood, and a piece of bread to symbolise wealth, warmth and plentiful food.

Before he enters the building, a window should be opened to allow any old bad luck to blow away. If a fair-haired man or woman of any complexion is the first to enter, members of that family will have bad luck. The person who makes this first-footing must leave by the same door he or she (preferably "he") entered or all the expected good luck will leave with them.

❖

Bells were rung, not to ring in a New Year but to commemorate the death of the old year just finished. Elsewhere, the Anglo-Saxons of old would scramble up on to their roof to see what the New Year was about to bring in. Some people still clean their chimney so that good luck can come into the house that way.

❖

Most folk still stock up their cupboards and ensure every pocket of what they wear on that evening has something in it. It is thought that an empty cupboard or pocket portends a year of hardship. This is also seen in the habit of banking up the fires on this night to ensure warmth and comfort in the coming twelve months. If these fires should go out before the next dawn so will the luck.

❖

Don't lend anyone anything from your house on the first day or you will give away your own good luck. Settle debts or they will double, perhaps one origin of the old saw "wiping the slate clean". He who drains a bottle from which others have drunk will have the better fortune. A New Year's Day baby has always been thought to be especially lucky in many countries.

Tradition has it that depending on which day the New Year starts shows us what to expect for the coming twelve months. Thus, on a Sunday it will be reasonably lucky; on a Monday, changeable; on a Tuesday, a tough time ahead; on a Wednesday, more travel than average; on a Thursday, many new experiences; on a Friday, a positive romantic time while on a Saturday, one must expect plenty of hard work.

The idea of New Year resolutions were originally superstitions started by the Romans to ensure good luck. They would make sacrifices to Janus (from where we derive the name of the month of January) to appease him and give expensive presents to their relatives. It soon became the law to include the emperor in these gifts but then they were thought of as a kind of tax.

Just about every day and date in the calendar has a history associated with it, apart from the many legends regarding their sequence and their names. Here are just a few that stand out as well as some little known beliefs and superstitions.

DAYS AND DATES

Each day has a planetary ruler. The Sun rules Sunday; Monday is ruled by the Moon; Tuesday by Mars; Wednesday by Mercury; Thursday by Jupiter; Friday is governed by Venus; leaving Saturday to the domain of Saturn.

To ensure good luck, one had to make obeisance to the god or goddess of each day. Gifts ought to be something ruled by the lord of that day.

SUNDAY

Sunday is ruled by the Sun and, as such, is a fortunate day for almost all activities. However, you should not change the sheets on the bed, don't cut your nails or have your hair done. Mothers with newly born babes should get out of bed together for the first time. If you sneeze before breakfast you will soon enjoy an affair of the heart.

Gold may be worn, but other jewellery must be kept to what is necessary or practical. If you sow or knit on a Sunday the Devil will drive your needle(s) and cause trouble. Do not begin or end a romance; don't play cards or even touch one when you put the pack away.

You must not gather in fuel for fires for any work done on Sunday will be undone on Monday. If away from home, do not start the return journey after dark. Even today in some fishing communities Sunday was thought an unsafe day to set sail. For many years sailors have had a fear or a worry about sailing on a Sunday almost as much as a Friday. Business deals were considered by many to be unsafe and, in parts of central Europe, it is believed a deal made today may not be legal.

However, it is a good day on which to marry or give birth, for Sunday's child will never want. It is still considered an ill omen to allow any grave to be left open on a Sunday for an early Monday morning burial. It should be completely covered..."lest the devil gets in and waits..."

MONDAY

Monday was once regarded as a barometer of the week for, if it rained, the rest of the week was expected to be dry. Weddings on a Monday were not particularly lucky because, even today, especially in Europe, it is widely believed to be unlucky to enter into any kind of agreement for business or pleasure on this first day of the week.

You must not ask a favour, borrow anything or make a loan. The first Monday in April, the second one in August and the last one of the year have long been considered as very unlucky indeed. Time decrees that they correspond with the dates Cain is alleged to have been born. Sodom and Gomorrah were destroyed and the birth date of Judas Iscariot was on a Monday.

It is very unlucky to turn a bed, or re-cast the mattress on a Monday. If out, and you meet with a flat-footed person you should return home at once, have a small meal, and then set off again. In Wales and the West Country babies born early in the day live longer and there is an old saw that goes "the later the hour (of birth), the shorter the life." One should never cut a new-born baby's nails before he (or she) is twelve months old – especially on a Monday!

TUESDAY

Ruled by Mars, the God of War, Tuesday was about the best day of them all to begin a battle or sue for peace – provided you had the upper hand, of course. Business affairs started on this day should go well as should any sporting event. Marriage was lucky for men but thought as unlucky for the women.

❖

The ladies should hold back from using any sharp instrument; the men should attend to the fires and neither should consult with a doctor nor undergo an operation. Flowers must not be cut or presented on this day nor should they be worn as adornments.

❖

Tuesday's child is either solemn and sad, or fair of face depending on where you live. It is considered to be a good day to cut your nails or have your hair cut. It is widely believed in the north of the UK that the woman who cuts the nails of her right hand with her left hand on a Tuesday will rule the roost once she is married.

❖

To meet with a left-handed person is unlucky. The ancient Norse God of Mischief Tiw, from whom Tuesday was named, was himself left-handed and it could be him in disguise.

WEDNESDAY

This day is ruled by Mercury, therefore travel should be fortuitous for business or pleasure but one must not wear gloves nor handle money. One may write letters and visit the doctor or start treatment but not when or if there is a New Moon.

It is a good day on which to be born in this country and abroad among the Moslems. In America, it is generally regarded as a most auspicious day. On the European continent, this is a largely unfavourable day, although almost everywhere it is widely believed a good day to be married – but not if there is a Full Moon. If sunrise is obscured by cloud, expect storms. "Hot" Wednesday is a reference to one particular day in July 1808 when the temperature reached an all-time high. As we didn't keep records in those days, we cannot be sure what the temperature did reach but it was apparently almost impossible to work, rest or play. Since then, in the mid-southern counties of England and in the London area, any unusual or extreme event that occurs on a Wednesday has been known as a "hot" time. The expression of "a hot time on the old town tonight" stems from this phenomenon.

To sneeze on a Wednesday before breakfast or after dinner is a sign of good health and longevity. It is one of the better days to marry, but not in May or on the "unlucky days" of any month.

THURSDAY

Ruled by Jupiter, Thursday abounds with superstition and beliefs the world over, with many of them quite contrary in their statements. In parts of Britain and Germany it is thought to be an unlucky time while in America and the Middle East it is a most favourable period. It is good for starting and finishing projects or dealing with difficult people. A very high proportion of monthly magazines and new books are published on this day in the British Isles.

One should not wear jewellery, especially red stones, as against gold or silver. People should not work in their home or garden but, if it is not a practical matter, then all work should be started in the hour of Saturn before dawn, and which ends at daybreak. When that particular hour begins depends on the time of the year, of course.

❖

The last Thursday in November in America is Thanksgiving Day but it was only in 1941 that it was declared a national holiday. Prior to this, the Aztecs and Mayans also used this day for sacrifices to the sun god for their crop yields. Maundy or Shere Thursday commemorates the king's generosity in the UK when he "allows" people to "beg" for his charity.

❖

A number of people, limited to that of the ruler's age, receive coins and food in an annual ceremony generally called Maundy Thursday. Superstition has it that, if the ruler fails to do this, the realm will fall.

FRIDAY

Ruled by Venus, Friday is rife with superstition and belief and is not the most favoured of days. Convicted criminals were usually executed, here, in America and on the continent. Sailors hate to begin voyages. In Hungary, when a child is born, a few drops of blood must be taken from the birth cleaning materials. The child, whether a girl or a boy, will be unlucky all through life. In many countries, pregnant women have a strong dislike or even a fear of going into labour on a Friday.

❖

Christ was crucified on a Friday and right up to the early 20th century many blacksmiths refused to work because (allegedly) one of them had made the nails for His cross. In Ireland, a blacksmith has always been regarded as being a particularly fortunate pursuit because work rarely dries up for them.

Farmers and gardeners (and even gravediggers) will not push any metal object in to the ground for much the same reason. But elsewhere, however, anything sown today will yield plentifully. It was on a Friday that Eve tempted Adam for the first time. Many women will not marry, start a new job or move house – especially in Spain, Italy and Portugal on a Friday.

❖

Many people all over northern Europe still hang a loaf on the wall that has been especially baked on Good Friday to offset illness and disease for the coming year. provided it is left alone. In Scandinavian countries, wood from mountain ash trees gathered in on Good Friday is placed around doorways for much the same result.

SATURDAY

This really is a day of mixed fortunes. Ruled by Saturn, better known as the Grim Reaper in some places, one must tread very carefully to appease the ancient gods who were thought to influence your future prospects. It was considered to be good for making journeys to places you have never been to before or for leaving hospital after your treatment is complete.

❖

Dream interpretation is most fortunate if carried out today because, especially in parts of Scotland, it is widely believed that those born today can "see and communicate" with those who have passed on. One should not employ new staff or have them start work on this day. In India, Saturday is not one thought of as one of the best of days for it is widely believed ruled by the gods of misfortune.

❖

Remember to not cut your nails or your hair. Attend a wedding as a guest but the actual date of the month determines whether it is lucky to wed or not. However, in these modern times, this is by far and away the easiest of days on which to marry because most people don't work.

There are many other old sayings, beliefs and superstitions regarding the individual days of the week, many of which are variations on what is written here. For example, you should cut your nails or your hair for good luck or ill on certain days but much depends on where you live as to the precise nature of the fortune.

◆

There is an ancient rhyme for babies and the day they were born, again with variations on a theme dependent on the area in which you live but all of which contribute to the rich tapestry of superstitions and beliefs the world over.

Thus, with all variations considered, the rhyme is as follows:

> Monday's child is fair of face,
> Tuesday's child is full of grace;
> Wednesday's child is full of woe,
> Thursday's child has far to go;
> Friday's child is loving and giving,
> Saturday's child works hard for its living;
> But the child that is born on the Sabbath day,
> Is bonny and blithe, and good and gay.

THE MONTHS

During any of the twelve months of the year and on certain dates in any one of them, there are many special occasions. Some may have religious or Pagan connotations while others have other reasons, like the time of the seasons, for example. We opened this chapter with New Year festivities and beliefs.

This journey though the months will reveal some fascinating thoughts as we proceed.

For example, one very little known superstition regarding January 6th, Epiphany, equating to the time when the Magi came across the Holy Child with their gifts, still takes place in some parts of the country. The master of the house must take a freshly baked loaf and, in front of the entire household, have it blessed. Then everyone visits each room passing the loaf among them as they proceed. Failure to do this meant the household would show little, if any profit at the year-end.

❖

On this Twelfth Night (from Christmas Day) all decorations must be taken down and destroyed. In the old days these were made mostly of natural materials. Today, these items are usually artificial and cost a fortune. Largely because of this, many can be and are re-used at the next Christmastide.

In some parts of the UK and in Northern Europe they had to be taken down and removed by Plough Monday, the first Monday after Epiphany. It is still thought to be extremely unlucky if this is not done, for members of the household would be unfortunate for the rest of the year.

On January 22, winegrowers in parts of France, Spain and Portugal will openly scan the skies for rain clouds, for this is St Vincent's Day, the patron saint of the winemaking fraternity.

❖

Good weather today implies a poor year for wine. Traditionally, cloudy or bad weather means a good yield for, "...if on St Vincent Day the sky is clear, more wine than water will crown the year..." If this day is a Thursday, then the chances are it will rain because in many European areas this is often the wettest of the week.

❖

In Ireland on February 1, St Bride's Day, oatcakes had to be cooked and eaten but the oats to come from the last of the previous year's yield.

This is also Candlemas Eve, for February 2 is Candlemas Day, and on this day all old candles had to be used up. In some areas in Europe and in the British Isles, where Pagan loyalties still abound, it is celebrated as one of the thirteen great Sabbath (or Sabbats) days of the witches.

In others areas, an old Pagan ceremony was carried out for the purification of all women, perhaps more to those of childbearing age. This was to symbolically cleanse them from the sins of the previous year and to bless and prepare them for being fruitful in the coming one.

❖

In parts of the USA, this is also known as Groundhog Day, an old Pagan or solar holiday. It was hoped that geese would lay the first eggs of the year. If they did, all would be well in the coming seasons. If they did not, then a lean time for all seemed to be the alternative.

❖

February 14 marks St Valentine's Day for lovers all around the English speaking world and whole books have been written about its potency in this world. However, few know that you should also make a wish as you eat home-made plum "shuttles", small buns made with dough, caraway seeds and currants. You must tell no one of what you wish for or you will never meet with your future spouse.

A very old belief is that this is the day that birds will choose their mates for the coming year. Such is the stuff of legend and superstition that all manner of beliefs have grown up around it all and added still more special spice to the day.

❖

This day also reflects the old Roman festivities in which young men could select a young girl with whom they could celebrate the occasion. Such chances did not happen very often like this, to be able to enjoy a party with the girl of your choice. One can almost see how the whole concept of St Valentine's practices has evolved in modern times...

❖

Youngsters would visit houses and would sing little songs in much the same way as those who salute Halloween or the Christmas carol singers do in these modern times. This was all performed in the name of good luck because in many rural areas it was widely believed that these acts would help those who work on the land to be successful.

Also, for reasons now long lost in the mists of time and certainly long before St Valentine came on the scene, it is also the day that farmers must start sowing their spring crops if they are to get a good yield, make a profit and be successful.

❖

Many farmers used to go church and pray for good weather to help. Others used to kneel and pray by their plough before marking the first furrow. In Berkshire, in the early 1940's when I was still a very young lad, I actually witnessed this happening.

❖

Shrove Tuesday, a moveable event determined by the date of Easter for each year, marked the time for the rural clergy to hear confession and give absolution to the local populace but this faded out shortly after the Reformation. More festive beliefs began to hold sway and superstitions have taken the place of the religious services.

Traditionally, making and eating pancakes is now a more popular event for the day. This dates back many centuries. It represents the belief that all the old food saved from the previous year must now be cleared away from the cupboards.

❖

Often, these would have been mainly scraps and left overs. The easiest way to get rid of it would be too cook it all up in a giant pot and wrap it in pastry made from remnants of the flour. Pasties, pies, omelettes and enormous pancakes were all concocted in the huge family pans.

❖

Some of these recipes of such times have come down to us in the form of the mince pies we eat today, perhaps more during the Christmas period. All this food had to be devoured before the following day, Ash Wednesday, the traditional start of Lent, which ends forty days later on Easter Day.

Almost everywhere, it was considered extremely unlucky to have anything left over from the previous year. If it were not possible to begin to exist on the foods that came in with the New Year that were slowly becoming available, then it was a very unfortunate affair.

If these efforts that people were making to sustain themselves were not enough, more hard work was needed. The fires had to be dowsed completely and then re-lit the following morning with completely new fuels. One should never light a New Year fire with anything from the old one. Those ashes were taken and spread on the ground as a mark of respect to Mother Nature and to symbolise that from dust we come – and to dust we return.

❖

March 1st, St David's Day ushers in spring for many in the rural areas. Leek pies had to be made and eaten, a superstition and traditional belief that is still followed all over Wales, of course. It is also still pursued in London, where the officers and men of the Welsh Guards have emblems in the form of leeks presented to them.

Those who cannot (or will not) wear a leek choose to sport a daffodil on their person. This is to symbolise and recognise St David and his goodness in those far-off days. He was also known as the Waterman in his day for he is alleged to have drank only water and, perhaps, a little milk at other times.

Because of this, there are still some Welshmen who will refuse to drink alcohol on this day as a mark of respect and also out of the belief that to do so would bring them very bad luck in the coming year.

❖

The 17th of the month, St Patrick's Day, has almost as many beliefs associated with it. He was responsible for the evangelisation and conversion of many old Irish beliefs. These matters are curiously referred to as the driving of serpents from Ireland. Superstition has it that snakes will not bite you on this day in Ireland. But if one should do so accidentally, there will be no long-term ill effects.

In Wales, wolves were said to be quite docile on March 17. Allegedly, it was St Patrick who changed the rebel King Verecticus into a wolf because he would not toe the line and that was his punishment. All Irishmen and women should wear a small piece of shamrock to mark the Saint's day.

❖

Lady Day on March 25 commemorates the Annunciation of the Virgin Mary and is also one of the Quarter days in England. Monies due for rent or other purposes must be paid at such times otherwise failure to comply could mean forfeiture.

In quite ancient times, this was the first day of the (civil) year and there is an old belief that if Good Friday or Easter Sunday should also happen on this date then within a year there will be a national misfortune or a series of similar events that (will) prove to be unhelpful to the UK.

In 1818 Lady Day and Good Friday occurred on March 25 and was said to have heralded the death of Queen Charlotte in the November. This was followed in 1819 by the Peterloo (Manchester) massacre of 11 people with some 350 or more injured when the cavalry charged into a crowd of protestors.

In 1853 this coincidence was followed later by the UK declaration of war against Russia, the Crimean War and the London cholera epidemic. The 1864 Lady Day and Good Friday joint date of March 25 is said to have heralded the terrible decision by the government to execute over 400 Jamaican rebels against the British.

❖

Good Friday fell on March 25 in 1910 and a few weeks later in May, the king, Edward VII, died. In 1951 March 25 fell on Easter Sunday. Within a year King George VI had died. Good Friday fell again on March 25 in 2016. On June 23 the UK voted to leave membership of the European Union if nothing else but to regain sovereignty over our own affairs.

The health of several members of the royal family was currently thought to be quite unhelpful but nothing untoward occurred in that area. The next time Good Friday falls on this date will be in 2103. In 2157 and then in 2187 this date will mark Easter Sunday.

❖

Astrologers who practised horary (event astrology) all felt that around this period there would be some major event that will involve London. The positions and aspects of some of the planets transiting London's natal chart on and from this date for a few months were, to say the least, a tad problematic. The UK vote in this matter was, therefore (and so far) quite an event and worth noting here. Finally, there is a very old belief which suggests that if anything really serious happens in or to London, then Liverpool will probably become the new capital city of the United Kingdom.

❖

Every year on April 1, All Fools Day, which most people think does not really belong to the realms of superstition, is actually celebrated the world over with hordes of practical jokers eager to demonstrate their abilities, one way or another.

❖

It all stems from India, certainly from Greece and even Rome and has its origins in Pagan ceremonies begun at the vernal equinox and which lasted for about a week or ten days or so. This period also coincided with the ancient New Year when all the superstitions and beliefs associated with such times began.

In ancient times it was thought that this was when Noah released the dove in its fruitless search for land. The French were thought gullible because they were fooled into thinking summer was early because of the warm days that can occur about this time. They left off their winter clothes and suffered as a result.

Others feel that the change of calendar in 1752 when the New Year was moved to January 1 is another answer but one that helps to perpetuate these ancient beliefs. When April 1, 1753 arrived many practical jokers tried to convince people otherwise with "odd" gifts in support and the idea caught on.

Traditionally, the fourth Sunday in Lent is Mothering Sunday, when all children were put to work in honour and respect of their mother. They had to present their mother with a small bouquet of freshly picked flowers, offer them a meal of roast veal followed with baked custard and a simnel cake.

This ancient piece of English happiness became heavily commercialised in the state of West Virginia when a Miss Anna Jarvis launched the idea of a proper Mother's Day in 1908. It became official in 1913 – and is celebrated on the second Sunday in May in that country.

❖

In middle England, Palm Sunday, the Sunday before Easter, is also known as Fig Sunday. This when we should all eat fig pudding to offset bad luck said to be liable to happen sometime in the next seven days. All cakes made on this day should have the mark of the Cross placed on them or they will not keep for very long. This could have started the hot cross bun idea. This start of Holy Week leading to Good Friday became a national holiday around the fourth century. Much superstitious belief and thinking abounds.

Anything sown or planted will produce a plentiful yield and many folk break a piece of crockery deliberately because it keeps the house itself safe. It is an excellent day on which to wean babies or animals for the first time.

Those who attend church in parts of Nothern Europe often take finger rings to be blessed to bring them good luck until next Easter. Some of these rings may have been made on Good Friday from the handles of coffins for they were thought to help make especially lucky emblems.

❖

Easter Sunday is a moveable feast day and is celebrated on the first Sunday following the Full Moon after March 21, the vernal equinox. Because of this simple little formula, almost 17% of the present Gregorian calendar is affected, for so many other dates depend on when Easter will occur each year.

One should always wear an article of new clothing to honour nature as she shows off her new green finery. Many people will have a display of

Easter lilies to symbolise purity. In parts of North and South America a bath should be taken by the elderly before daybreak because it is felt it will help cure rheumatism. In Germany it is thought the hare, sacred to the old goddess Estre, would lay eggs especially for the good children. All the fasting begun forty days earlier at the start of Lent ceased. Many people would get up early to observe the dawn for it is said the Sun dances as it rises on this day to commemorate the Resurrection.

Easter Monday merely extends the holiday period. Many games are played, many observances kept, many beliefs thought. Most are variations on a theme dependent on where people lived and could vary from neighbouring villages to the next town, city or county or country.

In all of these activities, the egg holds the most important place for it is the universal symbol of regeneration everywhere. The egg had been used long before the church took over the Pagan celebrations and tried to adapt them. Pace-egg rolling is played everywhere. The steepest local slope is used to roll fresh or hard-boiled eggs down. The last egg or the last one to break was the luckiest. If anyone cheated, it was very unlucky – punishment was severe and very painful.

May Day is celebrated with many beliefs because of the new crops, the cattle could safely graze on the new grass. The Druids used to celebrate May 1 as their New Year and all the rituals and beliefs associated with such times surface once again.

In 1649 the Puritans tried to end the superstitious belief associated with the very old Pagan maypole dances, which were largely phallic in their origin. When they lost power, those celebrations returned.

Young men had to go into the forests and woods to pick fresh flowers and greenery to present to their ladies and decorate their houses as a symbol of the season and its cycles. Young girls would rush to wash their faces in May Day dew for it was thought that it purified their skin and made them more beautiful.

Rogation Sunday is the fifth Sunday after Easter when it was believed that the crops must be blessed and the clergy were expected to do this, no matter what the weather. The next three days are Rogation days and precede Ascension Day. Largely religious in their origin, there are a number of beliefs regarding the time.

◈

Children were taken around the boundaries of their villages so they would not forget their limits and, as they went, they were "beaten" with willow branches to help them on their way hence the term "beating the bounds".

On this day also there were "well-dressing" ceremonies. All water-wells and their surrounds had to be cleaned and decorated with flowers for it is here that all manner of beliefs and superstitions abound. Wells were where one wished for portents of the future. Throughout history, oracles and other similar sites were kept immaculate for there could be no favourable portents, only misfortune if you did otherwise.

◈

Whit Sunday is the seventh Sunday after Easter and perpetuates the old myths that the rich had a duty to help the poor. On this day, those who were well off gave milk from their cows to the less fortunate. This was yet another excuse for feasting and making merry and teams of visiting Morris dancers would entertain the locals. In Scotland, this is also one of their Quarter days which may partly account for these gatherings.

◈

Midsummer's Eve and Day, June 23/24, is replete with superstitions and special beliefs. Both of these days fall within a very special period most associated with the Druids. The summer solstice is on June 21, the "longest" day, and they have celebrated this, most notably of late, at Stonehenge. This construction, whose altar stone has recorded the rising sun for centuries, was created long before they came on the scene. This is the best time to observe the fairies, to meet with elves or the goblins. It is a time of magic and superstition and to ask those mystic powers-that-be for blessings on your ambitions, hopes and wishes.

You should place St John's Wort around the entrances and exits of your house for protection from evil. Maintain fires all night. Outside, it is still a custom to burn bonfires all night all over the European continent for this is the time of light and sun worship.

Many young couples may leap through the flames hand-in-hand as a show of their love. Many modern witch circles treat this very old ceremony as symbolising the "marriage" of true lovers, a ritual I have witnessed on several occasions (I was asked to join one of these circles because of my astrological knowledge).

Some of the older village folk will sit in church porches all night to (allegedly) witness those who are destined to die in the coming twelve months pass through to make their peace with God. Young lovers will go to the local pond at midnight and look in the clear water for their future lovers who are supposed to appear.

Milk taken from cows on Midsummer Day should have a few grains of salt added in case witches had suckled from them and passed on their evil. Flowers picked today stay fresher and greenery lasts longer but if it rained in the night then nut tree yields may well be poor.

Hazel twigs picked today will be most efficacious for dowsing or water divining. This is, after all, midsummer, and from now on it is one long downhill slide to winter and Christmas again.

In July, the "dog days" run from July 3 to the 11th when Sirius, also known as the Dog Star, rises with the Sun. Often, they are the warmest days of the year. To fall ill during this period is fraught with incredible beliefs and superstitions. If it does not rain, fleas multiply, dogs go mad, snakes go blind and the noise they all make hurts people. Children should refrain from swimming because diseases from water are likely.

Everyone knows of the legend of July 15, St Swithin's Day, perhaps one of the most perpetuated of all the myths of yesteryear. If it rains, then it will continue to do so for forty days and nights.

On St James' Day, July 25, many people would (and still do so in many fishing communities) consume large quantities of oysters to ensure no one will want for money in the coming year.

❖

Lammas Day, August 1, was a quarter day in the United Kingdom but it is only observed now in Scotland. It was believed that all pasturelands should have the fencing removed to allow free rein for all animals to roam free – in many areas until the following spring. Unfortunately, many forms of rustling took place, so this activity has been largely discontinued. It is considered extremely lucky to use the first harvested grain to make a loaf of bread.

In some parts of the country, some say it should be consecrated to make sure the rest of the yield was high. Other factions insist it must be eaten. The word Lammas comes from an old Saxon word, "loaf-mass".

❖

September 14 is Holy-Rood or Holy-Cross Day. Young people and the fitter elders of the villages would go "nutting". However, it was also noted that high spirits might well lead to other activities. Young girls had to be chaperoned for "...the devil goes a-nuttin' on Holy-Rood Day..."

❖

September 29 is St Michael's Day, Michaelmas, is a Quarter day in the UK and also used to mark the renewal of servants in service for the coming year. As expected, prior to this everybody worked hard to make sure they kept their jobs! =

❖

Children and animals born at this time are believed to be particularly active and mischievous all their lives, for this was the day the devil fell to earth. His foot became entangled in a berry bush and turned the berries black – hence the blackberry.

It is a European superstition, rife in many places, that he sometimes returns to earth on this night to recruit helpers for his dark domain.

Perhaps one of the many reasons why some will not eat blackberries throughout the whole of the month of October, just in case...

❖

Elsewhere, the month of October was given over to hiring fairs, festivals and other communal or social events. It was also harvest time when crop yields and any surplus livestock were specially fattened to be bartered or sold off for necessary equipment and materials for the coming twelve months.

❖

Winter was also just around the corner, travelling was difficult, for the days were growing shorter. But it was still a great month socially and many old sayings and beliefs may be traced to this rather active period in the rural calendar.

❖

"Punkie Night" used to be celebrated in the southern counties, especially in Somerset. Punkies were actually the forerunner of the modern Halloween rituals in which "mangel-wurzels" (a large kind of beet) would be hollowed out to make lanterns similar to those made with pumpkins in the USA.

Youngsters who went calling for small gifts locally carried these lights. However, these activities have now been absorbed by modern Halloween night celebrations all over the world. This is largely where many superstitious beliefs and legends find their origins.

❖

Originally the last day of the Celtic year, this was the time for honouring those who had passed on. Some were thought to return to earth to make sure this was done properly. The Druids invited the spirits of the dead to return be examined to see if they might be re-born to live on in the body of an animal.

All Hallows Eve, the eve of All Saints Day, November 1, was once called All Evil Day and as it was believed to be given over to the living dead it was, perhaps, a better title for it. Pope Gregory IV attempted to discourage this by naming November 1 "All Saints Day" but legends and traditions like this live on mainly because such old habits and beliefs die hard.

The distinction between Halloween and All Saint's Day have now become so intertwined they are difficult to separate. Many of the old games, habits, beliefs and superstitions could have their roots here. Whether this was of a religious or Pagan origin or just a plain old tradition that started long ago, the real intention or reason has been lost in the mists of time.

❖

November 11, St Martin's Day or Martinmas, was one of the most important dates in the calendar. It is still a Quarter day in Scotland when rents, tenancy agreements, payment of accounts, loans and their repayments and other business matters were decided upon.

In some parts of Britain, some folk still call it "Rag-Pack" or "Pack-Rag" Day. Many servants would pack their meagre belongings and leave their employment for pastures new. Their new employers thought that they would get excellent service from their new staff for quite a few weeks. This was almost mid-winter when practically nobody in his or her right mind would want to be tramping the countryside looking for work at such a time.

❖

November 25 is St Catherine's Day. She is the patron saint of many rural and farming activities. The daughter of a Samaritan queen, she was put to death on a spiked wheel after unsuccessfully persuading a tyrant Pagan king to change his ways.

❖

Because of the way she died, wheelwrights, turners, millers and spinners pay her their allegiance. She is also the patron saint of spinsters. Incidentally, the Catherine Wheel firework is dedicated to her memory.

The Advent period begins four Sundays before the week of the Nativity. For fifteen centuries now this has begun the ecclesiastical year in the western Church and in many western countries two dolls representing the Holy Child and the Virgin are carried or displayed prominently during this time. In many places, people freely donate a small monetary gift as they pass.

❖

December 6 is St Nicholas' Day after whose original secret actions when he was said to have saved three young daughters of a luckless merchant from a fate worse than death. It is believed to be one of the (many) origins of why we give Christmas presents wrapped in such a way that the recipient should be unable to see what is in them.

It is alleged that he donated three small bags of gold, one to each of them in their hour of real need. From these charitable acts comes the origin of the pawn broker's three golden balls signifying that they secretly and honourably treat and deal with those who need help in times of temporary trouble.

❖

December 25 is celebrated as the birth of the Christ Child although it is now widely acknowledged that this cannot have been so. This date was given over for the Roman "Dies Natalis Invicti Solis", the ritual feasting in honour of Mithras, the God of Light.

❖

Just prior to this, from December 17, was the orgiastic Roman Saturnalia, a Pagan festival of Fire and Light and just after it came the Kalends of January for another three days and nights.

❖

As the empire spread so did the celebrations and they were, without any doubt, the wildest times of the year. To the Church, this represented a challenge and it was Pope Julius who introduced the Christian beliefs of the origins of Christmas in the fourth century.

Today, the Christmas period is a magical time for youngsters everywhere who have been brought up to believe in Father Christmas and all that he represents.

❖

It is a time of Yule logs, holly and mistletoe with plenty to eat. All these festivities derive from Pagan rites, many dating back hundreds of years. The Church in its long and tireless efforts to eradicate all the old Pagan beliefs, has carefully manipulated many of the old rites into the modern Christian rituals.

❖

Today, when we kiss under the mistletoe, we echo a once strictly Pagan ritual of greeting. It was a symbol of people who had to meet in secret to celebrate their rites. These were genuine believers who followed the old ways. Kissing the mistletoe or kissing under it proved they were genuine, for no one in their right mind would oppose the priests of these old orders, under pain of death.

❖

Mistletoe was and is widely used in natural healing and was thought to help improve fertility in women. When the Church would not allow it in their places of worship it began to spread to the ordinary household. Its presence suggested belief in Pagan ways and, over the years it has been gradually reduced in importance.

It began to be used in house decorations, lost in the other greenery, but there would always be a small sprig in the porch. People would be able to see the mistletoe on their arrival and the ritual greeting kiss would help to perpetuate the real meaning.

❖

Today, it is all but lost in most of the Christmas decorations, hung more or less anywhere. However, its origins live on in the sport of kissing under the mistletoe. However, it is still thought to be extremely unlucky to bring it indoors before Christmas Eve. It has to be removed by Twelfth Night, wrapped and disposed of carefully. It must never touch the earth under any circumstances or you will have terrible luck in the coming year.

❖

Candles are lit to symbolise light and warmth. But if one should go out, it is very unlucky for that household and for the person who lit it in the first place. In many places, here and abroad, cattle are said to turn to the east at midnight on Christmas Eve and, again, dependent on where you live, it is said they will bow. It is also thought by many that this may also happen on January 5, Christmas Eve in the old calendar.

❖

The belief that the Glastonbury Holy Thorn blooms on this day helps to perpetuate the myth that the real Christmas is on January 6. Cocks that crow on this morning help prove the point for it is an old superstition that it was a cock that announced the birth of Christ on this day. And in many areas of Europe it is considered extremely unlucky to kill and eat a cock that crows on this day.

❖

December 26, Boxing Day, is peculiar to the United Kingdom. The name is derived from church alms-boxes that were opened so that their contents could be distributed to the poor.

Other authorities suggest it may have something to do with apprentices' boxes which were carried around by them for their employers to show (or not), their satisfaction with them. Over the passage of time this has spread to all manner of services; newspaper boys and the tradesman, especially the dustman and milkman.

❖

This is also St Stephen's Day. This saint is alleged to have died in Norrtalje in Sweden, while some say it may have been the Middle East. He is the patron saint of bricklayers, those who work in the building trade and church deacons.

He is also concerned with horses and in some devious way is said to be involved with ancient ceremonial bleeding rituals on this date. Legend claims his grave was the source of many pilgrimages by sick horses – many of which were cured as a result.

Traditionally, there are many packs of fox-hounds that meet today and those dedicated to his memory do not hunt, they are only there for the meeting and not for hunting.

◈

December 28 is Holy Innocents Day also known as Childermas and is given over entirely to the commemoration of the children slaughtered by King Herod's troops. On this day, children everywhere are to be forgiven all their wrongs and should be indulged in their every whim.

Superstition has it that anything started today is doomed to failure. Curiously, very few ventures are launched at this time but then most folk prefer to wait until after all the New Year Celebrations are over... Which brings us all the way back to where we started.

Men and Women

As we grow older, we begin to realise that it is more or less expected of us to find a partner, enjoy a courtship, marry and raise children from the union. However, from a superstitious point of view, this whole venture is absolutely fraught with an enormous variation of beliefs and fears.

To start with, it has always been considered extremely unlucky for engaged couples to hear their own wedding banns read in church because, if they did, it was widely thought their children would not enjoy the best of health. In many rural areas it is still believed and expected of the oldest local person in the congregation to wish them well at the third reading. Once again, while growing up in Berkshire, I knew this procedure was pursued on several occasions. After this, the church bells might be rung as a special blessing unless they were to be tolled the same day for a deceased mother, in which case the future bride might not live to bear her first child.

This rather grim start to love and romance falters a little until the wedding day when, if you are superstitious, all manner of things can befall the bride and groom if they do or not do this or that first, second, last or whenever.

❖

The bride must wear a ring on the third finger of her left hand and it must be thrust firmly on during the ceremony or the bridegroom will not be the head of the house. Most European brides wear this ring on their right hand. The reason a ring is used is because of its circular shape, which it symbolises eternity and that their love is endless.

Nobody really knows the actual origin of ring giving and or the exchanging of them. We know the Egyptians used them well over 4500 years ago when they used rings made of rushes or reeds. They were more of a decorative or an ornamental symbol almost always worn by the women.

The ring is circular signifying eternity to these people and also to previous societies and cultures as well. For a man to present such a symbol to a woman was to show her his immortal and never-ending love. Unfortunately, these first rings soon deteriorated and were replaced first by leather versions, then bone or ivory.

The more expensive the material, the more love was being shown to the receiver. The value of the ring also demonstrated the wealth of the giver. The Romans had a different idea here. They gave the ring to show "ownership" of the woman and their rings were made of metal – probably iron.

This idea here fell into disuse and it wasn't until the middle of 800AD that Christians began to use rings in their marriage rites. However, the church disapproved of the rings that people used for they were more of a jewellery item and, in many cases, expensive but quite flashy. By around the middle of 1200AD the much plainer wedding band we know today began to be introduced into the marriage ceremony and even the church began to recommend the idea.

❖

It is not widely known that, when the priest invites the groom to kiss the bride, he is perpetuating the custom of earlier times when the couple were expected to have sex witnessed by all sundry. If this were not done, either family could challenge the "legality" of the union. Brides were expected to be virgins and if they were not it would lead to bloody battles in more than one sense. Thus, the couple had to perform. It is also one origin of the superstition that only the bride must name the wedding day – for more obvious and practical reasons.

In parts of Southern Europe guests waited outside the bedroom of a newly married couple to wait for the groom to show them freshly blood-stained sheets to enable "witnesses" to see that his new wife had been a virgin.

Such beliefs and acts have no set origin. It is believed that Cain, the son of Adam was the first man to use a ring to celebrate his nuptials. At various times during the history of men, women and marriage, it has been placed on the thumb, the index and, finally, on the third finger. One reason for this was because many of the ancients thought a vein went from this finger direct to the heart. Thus, when the ring is put on this finger it symbolically seals the union.

◈

Showering confetti is a belief carried forward from years ago when only the bride was covered in ears of wheat to symbolise a fruitful union. In Eastern areas rice was used instead. In these more modern times however, rice is used more and more so to help perpetuate the Eastern belief that the more rice showered on the happy couple, the more prosperous they would become. This was also expected to make her more fertile.

◈

The wedding cake is of a similar origin except that guests would bring small "bride-cakes" to symbolise and encourage her fertility. The origin of bridesmaids and the best man and his entourage are largely Anglo-Saxon. They served two purposes. They made sure the happy couple turned up and policed those who might not see or understand the politics or purpose of uniting the two families. The best man was only one of a group of "bride knights" who was originally expected to look after the bride prior to the big day.

◈

The bride was not allowed to be seen by anyone in her dress prior to the ceremony, now just limited to making sure her husband-to-be does not see her. She was not allowed to look in a mirror and was made to wear a veil in case an evil one saw her beauty, which is why many brides still wear a veil today.

"Something old, something new, something borrowed something blue and a sixpence in my shoe" is the correct ending to a rather long and quite old adage based on mystical matters from years ago.

"Something old" is obviously the past, when she was allowed to take very little with her into her new life. "Something new" was a small gift that was given to symbolise her new status. "Something borrowed" was a small loan from a well-established relationship to show she had good friends. "Something blue" in those far-off days represented purity to signify her virgin state. The sixpence referred to implies that she would also have brought a reasonable dowry to the union. I witnessed this ritual carried out in full in the mid 1960's at a wedding I attended in Surrey.

❖

It has long been believed that for a marriage to succeed a piece of the wedding cake must be sent to absent relatives and others to be included in the happy couple's new circle of friends as a mark of respect. In medieval times, bride knights used to fight for the honour of her garter; who ever won it was expected to live long and prosper.

However, this practice was eventually stopped by the Church because it opposed violence, especially in this gratuitous sense. Instead, the bride carries a small bouquet of flowers which is thrown to her maids in the belief that whoever catches it will be the next in line to marry.

The bouquet is also believed to symbolise the bride's wealth and status. Whoever catches it, therefore, also symbolically carries forward the same luck and rank when she comes to the altar and who is expected to do equally as well, if not better.

Even the wedding day speeches have a superstitious side to them. It was thought that, for as long as people listened to them, passing imps and lesser gods would enjoy the ribaldry and ignore the happy couple. Many centuries ago, people were hired especially just to do this but now such matters are left mainly to the best man.

❖

The honeymoon is simply a period of one moon to the next when all guests were expected to stay on to enjoy themselves. It was in this period that they drank wine, later mead and then honey while the couple were away.

The "honey-moon" was for the guests not the newly-weds. It has always been thought that to turn down an invitation or not to attend was a slight to the families. Even today, it is thought that if you receive a wedding invitation, it is considered extremely unlucky to turn it down.

The actual day of a wedding has influence according to many legends and beliefs. There is an old adage of what to expect dependent on the day.

❖

"Monday, for wealth; Tuesday, for health; Wednesday, the best of all; Thursday, for losses, Friday for crosses; Saturday, no luck at all."

❖

Even all those years ago, the Church rarely allowed a marriage to take place on a Sunday so there is no old saw to refer to for the Sabbath.

❖

A morning wedding has always been thought lucky because if no one broke their fast before the happy event, all could freely feast at the wedding "breakfast." Afternoon weddings allowed religious people to get up and go to church before the event to pray for the bride and groom. However, in many parts of the world, it was and still is considered unlucky to get married after sunset, for it was believed that any offspring might die before their parents.

❖

On the wedding night, the groom should ceremoniously lock all the doors and windows. Another very old belief is that whoever goes to sleep first on this night will be the first to die.

It is suggested the many May brides are doomed. This is the one month in which even the Romans would not marry, for during the whole month the dead were remembered and offerings made at various altars. Thus, no one in their right mind married then.

It was thought very lucky to marry at certain times and dates of other months, for it was believed that on these days the woman would be extra loving and faithful.

These were January 2, 4, 11, 19 and 21; February 1, 3, 10, 19 and 21; March 2, 5, 13 and 20; April 2, 4, 12, 20 and 22; May 2, 4, 12 and 20; June 1, 3, 11, 19 and 21; July 1, 3, 12, 19, 21 and 31; August 2, 11, 18, 20 and 30; September 1, 9, 16, 18 and 28; October, 1, 18, 15, 17, 22 and 29; November 5, 11, 13, 22 and 25; December 1, 8, 10, 19, 22 and 29.

These dates may vary slightly from area to area but there are also other lists that give the unlucky dates of the month – many are the same as these given above but they can also differ slightly depending on where you live.

❖

After all this fuss, wedding anniversaries have been celebrated in fine style the world over. Some have names, and presents to the couple should be of the material for that particular anniversary. Alternatives are in brackets and can vary slightly from country to country and area to area within a nation.

First	Paper
Second	Cotton
Third	Linen (Leather)
Fourth	Book (Fruit) (Linen)
Fifth	Wood
Sixth	Sugar (Iron)
Seventh	Woolen (Copper)
Eighth	Leather (Rubber) (Bronze)
Ninth	Pottery (Willow)
Tenth	Tin (Aluminium)
Eleventh	Steel
Twelfth	Silk (Linen)
Thirteenth	Lace (Moonstone)
Fourteenth	Ivory (Moss Agate)
Fifteenth	Crystal (Glass)
Sixteenth	Topaz
Seventeenth	Amethyst
Eighteenth	Garnet
Nineteenth	Hyacinth

Twentieth	China
Twenty-fifth	Silver
Thirtieth	Pearl
Thirty-fifth	Coral
Fortieth	Ruby
Forty-fifth	Sapphire
Fiftieth	Gold
Fifty-fifth	Emerald
Sixtieth	Diamond
Seventy-fifth	Platinum

As a rule, especially in those far off days, the first child would have been expected in time to celebrate the first wedding anniversary. It is here, perhaps, the reader should be reminded that life expectancy was a lot shorter than it is today. Few people lived beyond forty; fifty was a great age while anyone who lived to sixty or more was greatly venerated.

People used to marry in their teens which gave them a fighting chance of raising a family and establishing a happy home before their middle age set in. There was plenty of help in those days, for the community spirit was quite strong everywhere. Thus, as soon as it was known that the woman was pregnant, they would gather round to help and a whole new world of strange beliefs and superstitions were invoked.

It is now widely known abroad, but not so much in rural England, that the number of babies a woman might have was determined by the amount of teeth she lost in her first pregnancy. If two teeth were lost at the same time it was thought she would produce twins. However, many an expectant mother's first worry was about her child being premature. To prevent this, people would stand outside a house and throw stones over the roof. This extremely ancient belief has been dated to pre-Christian Greek times where stones were worshipped for all kinds of reasons.

Another problem was for when the baby would be born. Certain months were believed to help intelligence. For women, fertility or infertility was associated with some months and not others. Life expectancy was another, but good health or otherwise was a main worry for all.

❖

A Caesarean birth was greatly feared by both men and women and, in the light of what we know today, perfectly understandable. Hygiene was just a word in the olden days unless women attended the distressed mother. Their knowledge about such things was not just old wife's tales, but plain old-fashioned common sense and hard facts in so many cases.

❖

As a matter of interest, it is widely believed today that, because of our advanced medical abilities, a Caesarean birth often seems to lead to the child having a higher level of intelligence. In these operations, little if any damage can be done to the baby because there is far less chance of an injury. This belief has been largely supported by statistics.

❖

In most civilised countries many beliefs and superstitions have a range of possible origins while in primitive societies in parts of Africa or South America it just isn't possible to trace them at all. Nowhere is this better seen than in the last stages of pregnancy. As a rule, most men tend to opt out of anything to do with this, with a few rare exceptions. However, in the last forty to fifty years or so many men have begun to attend their women to keep them company and be generally helpful. Most hospitals seem to encourage this.

For most men it is something they will never forget and it does tend to help cement the relationship and bring them even more close to the mother of their child. Nevertheless, until it was all over, it was not that long ago when a man would travel quite fast in the opposite direction altogether.

In a few really primitive areas, a man was not allowed to see his pregnant wife as she would be taken by the other women and kept out of the way of society until she had given birth. In many of these communities the woman was not even allowed to speak her husband's name publicly (or privately), for it might weaken his strength and he could no longer hunt effectively.

At menstruation, many were expected to leave the family home until she was clear and men were not allowed to see, speak or in any way associate with her even to feed or render first aid in the event of an accident. She was greatly feared while in this condition and some thought she was cursed. Yet another possible origin of the term "the curse" used (mainly) by women today.

In many society organisations before, during and shortly after medieval times, men did not socialise much with women for they lived in a totally different world. At confinement they would want to know what sex the child was for they all wanted a son to carry on family name. In some areas a daughter would have carried some level of political punch for she could be married off to further an alliance.

❖

For centuries, astrologers the world over have been the most important player on the field at such times. If the prognosis was good then they, the children, reaped the rewards. If a negative outlook was forecast, then heaven help the child, male or female. In a few extreme cases it was not unknown to put the new-born infant to death.

In Western Europe we tended to treat our women and babies much better. In the United Kingdom there are still those who believe in the old adage of the day of birth. There are many variations on the theme.

"Monday's child is fair of face; Tuesday's child is full of grace. Wednesday's child is full of woe, Thursday's child has far to go. Friday's child works hard for a living, but Sunday's child is "loving and giving".

In our northern areas it is Friday's child who will suffer sorrow while Wednesday's child is quoted as "merry and glad". In rural Cornwall and Devon, Thursday's child is "meant for thieving". In fact, there are so many variations that if you were to assess them all, everyone or no one is lucky or unlucky. But then again, if anyone has the best chance, it seems to be Sunday's child.

In some England coastal areas this child cannot be hanged or drowned. In Scandinavian countries he or she may become a seer and unlikely to be bewitched. If any baby is born during the chime hours, that is, as the clock chimes the hour or quarter hour, it will be especially lucky. In Wales, it is widely believed that the earlier in the day a child is born the longer it will live because it is said, "the later the hour, then the shorter the life." A birth at dawn suggests success, while at sunset the babe is said to lack ambition and be lazy.

Those lucky enough to be born at the new moon can expect a good life, if at the waxing moon the next one will be the same sex while a waning moon presages the opposite. If born at the dark of the moon, it is thought it will not live for very long.

◆

Once a child is born, a completely fresh set of superstitions come into play. Any birth mark on the face can be licked away by the mother if she does it before she eats or drinks anything that day and she continues to do this, observing the same daily routine for as long as it takes.

If a baby is born with a caul, it is deemed to be very lucky indeed, for it can never be drowned accidentally or deliberately. This is one reason why a sailor set great store by possessing one. Midwives were known to carry on a brisk trade in such sales, for they secreted them without the mother knowing.

Sailors were known to pay a small fortune to keep a caul with them while they were at sea. In some Mediterranean areas it is thought that this trade still exists in some of the fishing communities. In very old times, lawyers and politicians endow the owner with eloquence and they would often seek the "Virgin's Vest" in much the same way.

A caul must never be thrown away or destroyed or the child will sicken or die. If it is thrown away, the fairies will claim it, in which case the baby will always do their bidding – and not all fairies are good!

◆

Twins or any other multiple births have interesting superstitions about them. In some primitive societies, if one of the pair was a girl, she may well have been sacrificed, whereas in other communities it reflected on the manly prowess of the father. However, in some parts of the world it is thought that when a woman bears two or more children at the same time it suggests she has been unfaithful for it is thought no man is able father two children at once.

After the birth some mothers may be cast out of the society to fend for themselves. In America, in the late 1970s, a father in California who would not accept that he could father twins sued his wife suspecting infidelity but she was adamant she had been faithful. Scientific tests proved he was the father of one but not the other. He won his case and later divorced his wife. In this particular case, and as a matter of interest, the father of the other twin was himself one of a set of twins.

However, despite this some folk seem born to have twins because just prior to the turn of the 19th century, one woman who died in Chester, Northern England, had given birth to 15 sets of mixed twins during her life!

Twins were thought to be favourites of the gods whether boys or girls, and as such were protected from harm by the local priests who would take them under their wing. When the time came for them to marry, especially if they wed their respective partners in the same ceremony it was a very auspicious occasion indeed.

❖

It has long been believed that all babies are born with blue eyes. This is not so. It is based on a faulty observation made many years ago. In fact, babies eyes may be almost any colour, but the cloudiness of the eyes usually make them look blue but as it all clears away the real colour becomes more apparent.

❖

To kiss a baby for luck is frowned upon by the medical fraternity because of the danger of germs but it has always been a popular moment in the east. These days people are more likely to "blow a kiss" from the hand. Superstition has it that the mouth and the lips are magical devices with strong healing powers because of the way the breath of life passes through. So when a parent kisses a small hurt or bruise in an attempt to ease the pain it is repeating this centuries old belief.

Babies must be baptised as soon as possible after birth or its soul may not enter heaven. When a child died before this could be done it would have to be buried in an unmarked grave in non-consecrated ground, its soul doomed to wander for eternity.

This grave was often on the north side of the cemetery where few people like to be buried. It is considered very bad luck to accidentally tread on such a grave so it was "accidentally" marked by a small bush or tree to prevent this from happening.

On some occasions the local priest would take pity on the dead child and allow it to be buried with an adult in a tiny coffin at the foot of the grave provided that members of either family did not dispute the idea.

This was one way of avoiding the superstition of the baby's soul being taken over. Stillborn children would be interred in this way, but only after the oldest member of the family had christened the child without benefit of clergy because the priest had been unable to get there in time. This would help the baby to rest in peace.

One must never allow a baby to see itself in a mirror before it is six months old or it will become prone to all childhood ailments. You must not trim a baby's nails with scissors until it is a year old. Father must bite the son's nails with his teeth, mother must do the same for her daughter or the child will become a thief.

In Ireland you must never rock an empty cradle for the mother will soon become pregnant again. Some say the baby will die before the next full moon. Throw the first tooth it loses into the fire to stop the devil or his helpers getting hold of the baby.

In many parts of America and middle European areas it is the custom to brush the baby lightly with a rabbit's foot before it goes out for the first time. This natural charm to help ward off injury through an accident should afterwards be tied securely to the child's pram.

❖

As the baby grows and matures into childhood it has to be taught what and when to wear certain clothes and to act without offending the evil spirits. First thing in the morning get out of bed on the right side or the side you entered it the night before.

❖

Put the right foot to the floor before the left and when you dress you must always put the right sock or stocking on first and then follow it right shoe or slipper. Then do the same with the left leg and foot.

❖

If you put anything on inside-out leave it like that for the rest of the day. Carry a proper clean handkerchief folded in a tri-corn shape, not a square. Should you inadvertently put a button in the wrong buttonhole as you dress, you should take off the whole garment, turn it inside-out once, and then try again.

❖

At breakfast, try not to accidentally or deliberately cross sharp-edged cutlery. If you drop a knife, you must let someone else retrieve it but you must not utter thanks. Spoons and forks must be very carefully dried after use because cutlery should never be left to dry on its own.

❖

We all know about bubbles floating in a cup of tea suggests money luck later that day. And if about to partake of the traditional English breakfast there is an old adage involving eggs that might help keep you safe for the day:

> "Break an egg, break a leg; Break two, your love is true; break three, then woe to thee".

While laying the table and you drop a knife then the first visitor will be a man. This represents the time when men would always carry a dagger or a knife, the Old Saxon scramasax, to help defend himself and to use at meal times.

Women never carried a weapon; they would eat with their man sharing his plate and his knife at the same time. Whoever drops a knife must never pick it up nor say thank you when it is restored to them.

Those people who are very superstitious often have a real fear of and a healthy respect for knives in particular. One should never give them a knife or a pair of scissors as a gift for they firmly believe it will help sever the relationship.

As a rule, if they accept anything sharp-edged like this in the first place they will insist on giving the donor a small coin as a payment to offset the problem as they see it. Some people keep a knife or an old razor blade under the front door mat to keep witches away.

If a fork falls to the ground a woman will visit the house. This again goes back to the same period when the first forks were introduced into English society at meal times in the middle of the 15th century. Forks were around for a long time before this, because the Greeks and Romans used them in their kitchens.

At first it was only the women who used the fork. She would dip into the meal with her fork and pick off little delicacies that her man may have cut or left for her and so the fork become synonymous with women. Many men did not use them publicly at first because they believed it made them look less manly.

If a spoon is dropped no matter where the baby is it will begin to cry. Never sweep or clean out a room for at least an hour after a guest has used it or bad luck will fall on that person. This custom is followed quite religiously in parts of Japan and other oriental countries.

❖

If you have to go out you should not look back or retrace your steps for whatever reason. If you have forgotten something, try to do without it if you can. If someone waves goodbye remember to respond with one wave only. They should not watch until you are out of sight but should start to do something else.

At breakfast, the breaking of the fast from the previous day, you never offer the salt to other folk you let them reach for it themselves. If you accidentally spill salt, take a small pinch and throw it over your left shoulder for that is where the devil sits. The action will temporarily blind him for a while and he cannot vent his spite.

Salt was a very precious commodity. Many people were paid in part with salt from which the word salary is derived and also the old saying that a man was not worth his salt. This indicated a lazy person or one who could not do his job properly. Salt was also used to forecast the weather for when rain is on the way, it becomes moist.

❖

Knives must never be crossed but have to be laid very carefully side by side on the table. This was not so much good manners but to indicate to a guest, whoever it was, that the host had peaceful intentions. In the bad old days if an argument arose a man was just as likely to plunge his knife into his opponent to settle the matter.

Thus, before and after any meal a knife and fork should always be laid neatly side by side on the plate and never crossed. Weapons left crossed everyone knew was a sign of hostile intent. To show they came in peace, many Americans and some European people tend to eat only with a fork, with the other hand clearly visible on the table.

❖

When cooking, and if possible, try to use stale or unwanted bread or otherwise break it up and feed it to the local wildlife. It has always been thought very unlucky to throw away bread. Special guests would be allowed to have the top slice of a loaf of bread as a mark of respect for the top of a loaf in ancient times was always the tastiest. This gave rise to the expression that, "he, or she, was one of the upper crust".

❖

You should always be careful that when you cut a loaf you never offer a slice with a hole in it. This is a "coffin", the long hole that occurs occasionally in a badly baked loaf. It is believed to be a sure sign of a funeral in the family within a year. Never put a loaf upside down on the plate or table and never have help to cut bread, for two hands on a loaf brings bad luck. It is unlucky to take the last slice of carved bread unless it is offered to you.

❖

Never sing before seven o'clock or you will be in tears by eleven and never sit thirteen to a table. In times of yore, most would-be hosts tended to invite fifteen or more to dine. In the event of someone failing to come it reduced the guests to fourteen which presented no problem. However, if two failed to turn up, then almost anyone would be found and made to sit at the table to ensure bad luck did not pursue anyone present. Most people hosted smaller affairs to ensure this never happened.

❖

Wine must always be served or passed clockwise or, in the old days, the way of the Sun. To do otherwise would be to tempt fate. This originates from ancient sun-worship religions and to pass wine around in reverse, widdershins, brings bad luck. When it does happen, it suggests someone present could be a moon-worshipper, one who deliberately does everything in reverse.

❖

Never tap a glass or make it sing. This means someone somewhere could be drowning at sea and the only way to stop it was to stop the noise by touching the glass, thus allowing the unfortunate one a chance of rescue. I can find no origin for this most unusual belief, except that references are more often found in superstitions regarding the sea and sailors.

❖

Prior to retiring for the night brings a lot more superstitious thought. You should always tidy up and put brooms back into their cupboards or the local witch may spirit them away. If she did take one to use, the whole house and the people in it were in danger for, if she were to have an accident and perish, then strange things would happen.

All lights should be extinguished and fires put out, windows and doors must be tightly locked to prevent the spirits of the night entering or roistering at your expense – much the same as today if you think about it. Always make the sign of the cross over the keyholes as you pass by as an added precaution.

❖

Depending on where you live, your bed should be aligned either on an east-west path or north-south. If you have sleepless nights, change the bed around and your rest will be more peaceful. This is actually practised even today in this 21st century. Make sure the bed "runs" with the floorboards, not across them or someone (including you) will have a hard and painful time dying in that bed. It is unlucky to turn the bed or change the bedclothes on Fridays and Sundays. Make the bed on your own; never with help, or there may be an accident in the home within a moon.

❖

Get into your bed exactly the same way as you got out that morning and as you intend to leave it the following morning, provided you manage to survive the night, of course. To ensure you do, always look under your bed to make sure there is nothing lurking there.

❖

Young girls in various Celtic areas always used to do this to make sure that neither they nor their current young man would come to any harm. People should not take a hot drink to bed with them, especially boiled water that will gradually chill during the night, for this upsets the devil. If he should pass and want a drink, cold boiled water will make him angry and he will leave his mark on you. Many Americans refuse to lay their hats on a bed because it brings bad luck. Unless you have an accident or are the victim of some other fate, you will probably end your days in your bed.

Those who dwell by the sea and are in their last throes know they will not pass until the tide begins to ebb and take their strength with it. The death watch beetle is supposed to be heard tapping away at these times and a dog that howls or an owl that screeches portend imminent passing.

❖

It is an old English belief that if someone is ill in the house and a picture drops from the wall, the end is near. In very old times, it was thought that death was contagious and those who enjoyed good health in a house where death was expected would dress in black to make sure they were as inconspicuous as possible.

❖

This belief gradually led to people wearing black for mourning. However, this is not the universal colour for such a time. In Eastern countries, like China and Japan for example, they wore white, and many still do.

❖

In Egypt they wear yellow, while in Iran they don blue vestments. These practices differ quite widely depending on where you are. In parts of South Africa red is worn, but in northern parts of Africa such as in Ethiopia, the people prefer to wear light brown. In Armenia violet is the choice.

❖

In some countries, the dead person is sat up in bed for the wake, which stems from the belief that until he or she is buried, they need watching to make sure evil spirits do not try to take their soul. This is another reason for all the heavy drinking and the noise, possibly the one being caused by the other most of the time. The noise is supposed to scare off any spirit that might want to try its luck.

❖

In many places all over the European continent and in the United Kingdom churches toll the death knell either with one bell, usually known as the Passing Bell. Others toll the Nine Tailors, which is a corruption of the nine "tellers" or strokes used to indicate death which, in those ancient times, were nine for a man, six for a woman, and three for a child.

❖

In France there is a superstition that the last person to be buried in any cemetery is doomed to wander the area until the next person passes. If that person is "seen" by anyone in that period, then he or she will be next to follow them to the grave.

❖

When a coffin is carried from the church to the grave it must be "with the Sun", that is, in the same direction as the Sun travels from the east to the west. If not, those carrying the coffin are doomed and the dead person may not rest in peace.

Social Life

In everyday life there are a host of strange superstitions which many of us might or might not observe as we go about the business of the day. We know what we should do while in the home so, as we actually close the front door to go out, we should also remember that there are many other little observations and beliefs to be observed to make our excursion safe. For example, as we leave, we should never turn our back on the front or back door until we are well clear of the house.

This goes back to when life was pretty cheap and there was always someone somewhere prepared to dispatch you for a penny or two. Most people tended to look in all directions before they set out just to be on the safe side.

However, it was rare to look along the walls of the house and, as he stepped out, the unseen enemy could strike. There was always an additional chance of the devil or one of his minions waiting to tap you on the shoulder and claim your soul when it was your turn to leave this world.

Protection against such practical dangers in these perilous times gave rise more to custom than superstition but time has exacted its toll in this area. Some semblance of luck (good or bad) has now crept into what it is believed that people should do.

For example, most men normally walk on the outside of a woman or at the very least on her right hand side, otherwise it will bring her bad luck. This may be traced back to when a man's right hand had to be kept free, ready to defend her by drawing his sword or dagger if they were threatened. While some men may have been left-handed, they would have been very few and far between, so what first became a custom is now a superstition. Also remember, left-handed people were not well regarded in olden times.

Other apparent dangers of the times, more in town than out, are far less obvious today. In medieval times in this country and many other European countries, houses were built so they became wider the higher they went. Buildings began to gradually develop into light open structures with more outward thrusts counteracted by a deeply projecting "wall" and light "flying" buttresses. People passing by were half protected walking under the "shelving" thus formed.

However, the time was when sanitation left a great deal to be desired for it was the custom to open the bedroom window and simply throw the contents of the chamber pot into the street below. There may have been a shouted warning at the time, but it would have been coincidental with the emptying of the pot.

Whoever happened to be walking past on the paving below at such a time suffered greatly the further from the shelter they were. This then, is one of the origins of the custom of insisting the lady should walk on the inside of her escort.

We tend to set out on our journeys these days well prepared for good or bad weather because we will have taken note of the forecast. Apart from knowing country lore regarding weather, in those days few had any idea of what to expect.

However, if, on the evening before, bats had been seen flying near the house, then the following day's weather would be fine until noon. But if it had been a red sun at the dawning, it was a warning of bad weather.

❖

A red sky at night is a shepherd's (or a sailor's) delight for it means fine weather the following day. If a thunderstorm, perhaps with lightning, was expected then people lit a fire in the grate. It is still a rather widespread belief that lighting will not strike a house if a lighted fire is in the grate, although very few would venture out without first making sure the fire stayed in, winter or summer.

❖

Today we know it is unwise to stand under a tree while an electric storm rages overhead but many people would, and still do, head for the nearest oak because it is believed it will afford a protection that other trees cannot. We are able to trace the roots of this to tree worship and, in particular, Druidism.

Oak trees have been planted by property owners for centuries because of these and other associated beliefs in the magic of trees. People still touch wood for luck all over the world because of the belief that gods lived in trees, especially oak trees in the case of the Druids and the Celts.

They were known to approach the tree, ask a question of the gods, and when their wish was granted they would return and knock three times on the bark in a gesture of thanks. Even today, many superstitious people will have wood from an oak used in any part of the construction of their home.

It is said that all trees have magical or special meanings and the oak is widely thought to mean or represent hospitality. When we look through some of the lists of these meanings, for there are always variations, we note the apple means temptation, while the aspen is associated with grieving. The elm means dignity, the hawthorn will yield hope.

❖

In some English rural areas newly-weds are given a small piece of carving from the linden, or lime tree to keep in the bedroom to symbolise long and happy conjugal love sessions.

❖

The cherry tree helps to confer knowledge, for it means education and the mulberry suggests wisdom; the poplar means courage and a pear tree means comfort. Alas, the willow has always represented mourning but one should have one in the garden or nearby for the bark can be and still is used to help alleviate rheumatic fever and other similar pains.

❖

However, we have now left home and are making our way to the shopping area. On the way, those we meet must pass us on our left side, for if trouble should strike then our right hand is free to seize our sword or dagger to protect ourselves.

There was no traffic to worry about, so people would mill about as they saw fit but most would have walked in the sunlight, for to walk in the shade could bring the devils of darkness out to seize them. Next time you go out, observe how many people prefer to walk where the Sun is shining, as against those who elect to walk in the shade unless, of course, they happen to want a shop on that side of the street.

◈

When out shopping, there are right times and wrong days for a number of everyday different wants and needs. Never try to buy fish on a Monday, for you will only be able to obtain stale stock because fishermen everywhere would rarely set sail on a Friday or a Sunday. That left only the stock from either the previous Thursday or Saturday's haul.

◈

Additionally, that was always considering there wasn't a new moon on the Saturday, in which case fishermen would have done their best to opt out of their sailing obligations. Those who would try to set sail on a Sunday had to hope there would not be a full moon – another superstition for not going to sea.

◈

If you were going to buy goods that normally have a long life, like bed linen, sheets or furniture make sure the Moon is waxing from new. Many people would consult with their local fount of wisdom, an old lady wise in the ways of such things or an astrologer if there was one nearby, always assuming they could afford his or (very rarely) her fees. Most country folk would have some knowledge of when the Moon's quarters were due and would wait until the most auspicious time for their shopping sprees.

◈

Even in these more enlightened times, we are advised of the best time to buy this, do that or whatever. For example, it is better to buy a fridge or tools while the Moon is in Aries because it is less likely to go wrong. Electrical tools should be purchased at this time as well. If these items are bought while the Moon passes through Cancer they may well develop faults. The fridge is likely to spring a leak and the tools could prove faulty because of poor workmanship.

Many people believe they should arrange their days with the help of the Moon because superstitions regarding her influence are legion, with whole books written about them. Many people refuse to travel over water unless the Moon is in Sagittarius or one of the Water signs such as Cancer, Scorpio or Pisces.

❖

Any purchase for the kitchen should be made while the Moon is passing through Cancer, the natural sign of the home. Computers, televisions, radios and CD players are best bought while she is in Aquarius and, curiously, clothes always seem to fit better when she is Taurus.

❖

Of course, our journey may not be to shop or trade but to attend church. Do check the roof before entering for, if there is a bird on the weather vane, there will be a death locally within the period of the next moon and some say it would be the next person to enter the church.

❖

If any bird other than a robin should fly into the church after a service has been convened, all will be well with those present. If it is a robin, one of the congregation will shortly meet their Maker.

❖

Try not to turn over a hassock even it is already on its side or upside down, or the next twenty Sundays will be unlucky. While in church, collect some of the dust, preferably from near the altar. You should take it with you if you intend to visit a sick or dying person. Sprinkle some over their bed and, it is claimed, the patient will soon be up and about again. Alternatively, it is thought that it will help smooth the passing of those who are really ill.

❖

In Germany, there was a belief that a dog should be made to enter a brand new church before consecration and then before the first christening. It was thought that the first living thing in both cases to enter the church is doomed to become a servant of the devil. Thus, when the animal came out again, it was destroyed but later buried in consecrated ground in recognition of its selfless act.

◆

It is extremely unlucky for married women not to attend a church service as soon as is conveniently possible after giving birth. If she should go anywhere else for any reason, she will bring bad luck to those with whom she comes into contact and she will be cursed. The lady might not have been made welcome in any house and could be refused entry in her own home even by her own family.

◆

This was known to have been observed as late as the 1950's in parts of central England, Lincolnshire and Oxfordshire and the Welsh borders. Also in these areas the woman's husband was not allowed to attend with her or, if he insisted, he would not be allowed to sit in the same pew. If he ignored this convention, neither he nor his wife would be able to produce any more offspring or, if any children were born, they would be sickly and soon die.

◆

If you were in church in Malta, you had to remember that where a church clock had two faces, one always showed the right time, while the other deliberately showed the wrong time. This was done to confuse the devil and his satanic assistants. In this particularly superstitious small country, it was believed that it would confuse the evil ones and that they would never know when to come to church to hunt for fresh souls.

◆

If your intended journey was to a hospital, you would never take red and white flowers with you, for they symbolise blood, bandages and death. Doctors and nurses in particular would whisk them away to the hospital chapel. While in the ward, you should not move a chair in case you knock it over, as this presaged bad luck for the next patient in that room.

Nurses who made beds carelessly or left bedding over the back of a chair if temporarily called away on other duties were helping to speed the death of the most seriously ill in the ward. To put a patient into the bed of someone who had just died implied he or she would suffer the same fate. To avoid this, the bed was moved to a new position but in the same ward.

Some superstitions cast doubt on the colour of some medicines and pills. Anything pink was acceptable, the normal healthy skin tone. Red or blue suggested a potential blood infection. Black presaged death and had no place in any treatment. It many places in America it is still thought unlucky to enter hospital on Mondays or Wednesdays but good luck on Tuesdays and Thursdays. There are many variations of this belief these days in Europe and the UK. To leave on a Wednesday is considered to be the best, while Saturday is thought very unlucky, for it is expected that you may soon return for further treatment.

You may have made the journey to dine out, in which case you should wait for proof of any trust between you and your host. He should first pour two drinks from the same container and down his before you touch yours. After a short wait you may drink your own, for all will be well unless, of course, he is wearing a ring or rings. Superstitious folk often wear rings or have a fear of wearing a ring on the wrong finger or hand. In medieval times and much later, a doctor would wear a ring on his thumb. Many a general merchant and other business folk wore a ring on their first fingers.

Those who wore a ring on their middle finger were superstitious and often not very well educated. Somebody who wore a ring on their third finger might have been a student. For centuries, lovers have worn rings on their little fingers and from about 1720 or so, and because King George I had such dreadful taste, wedding rings became so heavy and ornate they could only be worn on the thumb.

However, toward the late 17th century a ring worn on the little finger used to be called a "Surprise Ring". The "surprise" was that the ring had a hinged surface made to turn over at a touch to reveal either a magical or "secret" design. There would also have been space for a small quantity of poison to be in the cavity.

❖

An adept would have found it very easy to drop poison into a guest's drink without being seen. Over the last two hundred years or so people have translated this belief into superstition, with some vindication in certain circumstances, and this is why many may refuse the initial offer of a drink until they have taken the opportunity to sum up the situation first.

❖

In some oriental countries it is the accepted custom to politely refuse the first offer of food and drink because of this belief. However, when salt is a part of the first offering it should be accepted immediately without any qualms because of the very high value put on this commodity.

❖

When you are about to actually eat certain foods, there are a few very special beliefs and superstitions that ought to be observed. Fish should always be sliced toward the head end. When eating an egg, break the shell into small pieces, for witches will try to obtain it for their recipes. When disposing of the bits of shell after the meal, they must never be burned, for this will stop the hen from laying more.

❖

To find out if your host or guest is a liar, politely ask them to cut a few slices from a loaf of bread. If they cut uneven slices they should not to be trusted and if the bread crumbles in your hands an argument will break out. If you are to keep lucky you must finish the meal with cheese and refuse anything afterwards for as long as you are in the house as a guest.

If your journey was to visit a cinema or a theatre to see a film or a show, you must be on time and try not to enter late. You should sit in an even numbered seat and refuse all attempts to make you do otherwise. Unless you have reserved a seat, avoid row "M" (the thirteenth letter) and the number 13.

❖

Less than two hundred years ago, formal schooling was quite different but, somehow, these childhood beliefs and superstitions have been perpetuated through the years and are as fresh as the day they were first told. As you read through just a few of them no doubt a few memories will be stirred.

❖

There are so many variations on what you should do when you see a white horse but the general consensus is that you must spit three times over your left shoulder, make a wish and say: "White horse, white horse, you bring me good luck". In Northern England you must then look for a red headed girl if you are a boy but if you are a girl, look for a red-headed boy to consolidate the wish.

❖

All possible bad luck seems to come in threes, superstitions carried in to adult life probably as a matter of course. If you hear of a birth, it is said you will also hear of a marriage then a death. Should you hear of two births, marriages or deaths you will almost surely hear about the third before dusk.

❖

Ambulances feature strongly with children's beliefs in central English counties. To offset being a passenger, people tuck their little fingers inside their palms until it has passed out of sight and hearing. It is also thought in some Celtic areas that your fingernails will drop off.

In southern areas they may also say something like, "Cross my fingers, cross my toes, hope I don't travel in one of those". Others will hold their collar until they see a four-legged animal unless it is a black cat, in which case they will have bad luck.

The ambulance is a relatively new idea but the crossing of fingers and the fear of black cats is as old as the hills. The former is obvious; making the sign of the cross has long been a traditional way of fending off trouble from any source. A fear of black cats goes back to medieval times when they were thought to be a witches' familiar.

❖

If a bird's droppings fall on you it is thought very lucky indeed but to see a white bird is thought to be most unlucky. One must never walk over a bridge as traffic passes underneath nor walk under it while the traffic passes over at the same time. These days there really is a problem with either idea.

❖

Children have a fascination with ladybirds. To find one is thought to be especially lucky on the day and no child would ever dream of hurting one for fear of the wrath of just about everyone. Magpies bring good or bad luck depending on where you are and how many are seen:

"One for sorrow, two for joy, three for a girl, and four for a boy",
runs one version, while another saying maintains:

"One for sorrow, two for mirth, three's a wedding, four for a birth".

❖

It is important to speak the rhyme out loud for a fear of incurring bad luck. In many areas, the magpie has always had an affinity with good or bad luck. It is essential, therefore, that you remain on good terms with them at all times. This is repeated with crows, cuckoos and doves, dependent on where you live and the local beliefs.

❖

Many children fear nuns, especially those in full habit and if the nun is walking away from them. When a nun walks toward a child, especially in strongly Catholic areas, many children will be seen to make the sign of the cross then they will open and close their coat.

In almost all rural and coastal communities in the British Isles children love sailors and many of them will try to touch his collar. In France, to touch the red pom-pom on a sailor's cap brings extra good fortune, but only if he is wearing it at the time.

❖

There is a very strong belief perpetuated by children in all built-up areas to never tread on the cracks between paving stones. To do so will bring all manner of strange ills, bad luck and general misfortune for the rest of your life.

It is not unknown for adults to avoid stepping on these gaps to prevent ill-luck and even the great General Gordon of Khartoum was seen to avoid them like the plague when out walking in the streets of London or other cities.

❖

Perhaps you went out to go to a club to play a game, tennis, a swim, or an indoor affair like darts, cards or bingo. There are many variations on the beliefs of good or bad luck involved here. Almost all ball games have a degree of luck involved in them and many are absolutely riddled with superstition.

❖

One of the many cricket superstitions is that you never try to take a quick single, however easy, because if your existing score is 12 then you don't want be on 13. It is very unlucky to clean off dirty leather ball marks from your bat because you will wipe away your luck.

❖

Quite a few sportsmen have special little talismans they always carry to ensure a good score. They range from the traditional mascot, like a rabbit's foot through to one man who once found a coin on his way back to the pavilion after a very successful innings. He never batted again without it.

In a game of tennis, for example, it is thought to be very unlucky to re-use the same ball with which you have faulted on first serve. To use it suggests you are encouraging bad luck. Players would discard the ball and not play it again, certainly in that game. In badminton it is felt that whatever end you win first has to be your lucky end. You have only to lose once at the other end for the jinx to come into full play against you.

❖

Football is riddled with superstition. In fact, there is as much on the field as there is off. Some footballers believe they play at their best only when they have brand new laces in their boots. If they are right-footed, then the new laces will be put only into the right boot; if they are left-footed, then only the left boot would be given a new lace. One man feels he is unable to play properly unless he runs on to the field fourth in line when the team first runs out.

❖

Some teams have a child mascot in full colours who has to be first on the field and carrying the ball before the captain. He then passes the ball to the oldest player who must pass it to the youngest. A goal-keeper likes to touch both sets of goalposts before the game starts.

❖

Supporters tend to play their part as well, if some press reports are to be believed. One man would wave his pools coupon up the chimney before posting to ensure that both he and his team won – he never marked them for a draw, only a win.

❖

One team won after a few supporters dressed up as angels. On the second occasion they won again, so the supporters continued religiously for a while but then the team lost. Some felt they had been tempting fate by dressing in such a fashion, while others argued for different causes. In the end, they went dressed normally – and the team won!

SUPERSTITIONS

The sport of kings has its fair share of beliefs and superstitions. To start with, once a horse has been named, the owner must never change it or it will bring bad luck not only to the owner but on all the staff who work at the stables as well.

❖

Jockeys are among the world's worst for superstition. They insist that their boots must never stand on the floor but should always be laid down side by side. Colours are very important as well in the racing world. Green is by far and away the most unlucky almost everywhere. Amulets, talismans and all kinds of lucky charms bearing personal favourite colours are carried in pockets, inside hats or under their silks. Never wish a jockey good luck before a race or he is likely to have a fall.

❖

A horse with four white feet is said to be very unlucky but one single white foot is lucky as is a horse with one white foreleg and one white hind leg. A white horse is not always lucky, if you see one, spit and make the sign of a cross in the dirt. In America it is considered to be extremely unlucky to see a white horse ridden by a red-headed woman.

❖

All over Britain, plaiting a horse's tail began because of superstition. It was thought that coloured ribbons woven into its tail made it safe from the devil. To ensure this, a priest would have to supervise the work. Today, plaiting is done more for style and convenience. However, if you want to be a successful gambler with horses, you should make your selection with a pin once used to help make a wedding dress. It is thought to be infallible.

❖

When it comes to cards, and in particular gambling games, beliefs and superstitions fly everywhere. They all probably stem from the cards themselves where a wealth of recorded material is readily available. Ordinary playing cards and tarot cards, "The Devils Books" as they are known almost everywhere, are credited as an invention of Satan.

It is said he always hides under the table ready to claim his victims as they win or lose. He wins either way because the winners become addicts while losers have been known to commit suicide on the turn of a card. And the devil is always there to collect the soul.

❖

Miners would not allow playing cards down a mine, sailors abhor them on board ship and even sneak-thieves would leave them alone as they thoughtlessly looted premises. To them, it was thought that they would be taking a gamble on being caught.

❖

To meet a woman on the way to play cards is unlucky. If she happens to be cross-eyed then she has the evil eye so you might just as well turn round and go home because you are not going to win anything that day. Many men will not play cards with cross-eyed men for the same reasons.

❖

How the cards are cut, where a player sits and how they actually gamble, all allegedly have their effect on luck. When you have a run of bad luck you should change your seat. Turn your chair round, right to left, never widdershins or you will lose even more. If you still cannot win, stand up and play. If that doesn't work, sit on newspaper placed between you and the chair. If you drop a card during a game, and not the interval between games, call for a new pack to change your luck. The list of potential luck-bringing exercises is endless. When you learn the meanings of cards in fortune-telling exercises it becomes easy to understand why there is so much folklore attached to them.

❖

Died-in-the-wool gamblers go to extraordinary lengths to win or put a hex on their opponents. They will surreptitiously place a match in the ashtray. A few moments later they will place another one it to make the sign of a cross – symbolically crossing-out their luck. Wily opponents who spot this use their cigarette to displace them.

In the USA, South Africa and Western Europe, if the ace of spades is dropped, on its own or with others, the game becomes forfeit. Many players refuse to play on for they take this as a signal to stop. When playing roulette in a casino, superstition is equally as rife. One of the saddest beliefs is that if a man does commit suicide because of heavy losses, play will continue in the belief that a human sacrifice will appease Lady Luck and it is right to carry on.

The expression "to play a hunch" comes to us from ancient Egypt when a dwarf cult existed and it was believed beneficial to touch the hump of a deformed man (not a woman) for luck. In the Middle East some men still wear a special amulet dedicated to this original dwarf god for luck.

Dominoes seemed to have made their first appearance in the middle of the 1700s in Europe near the borders with the South of France and Northern Italy. Certainly, those made of bone were observed about this period but no one is quite sure how, when, where or why they really originated.

Returning prisoners-of-war had sets and they seemed to have treated them as an advanced form of dice. These people would have no money with which they could gamble so, perhaps, dominoes evolved as an alternative which shares many of the old dice superstitions.

A standard set of dominoes contains twenty-eight rectangular tiles that are divided across the middle by a line. Each half may either be a blank or a number and they start with a double-blank through to a double six. The value of each tile, therefore, depends on their spot value. So, a four-three tile is worth seven and so on. Odd-numbered tiles are considered more favourable than those with even numbers, especially when used for telling fortunes, along similar lines to dice or playing cards.

Red-coloured pieces are shunned in middle European countries with black and white being the most popular elsewhere. From the early part of the 20th century Bakelite and, latterly, plastic has replaced the old style bone and ivory sets.

It is believed that dominoes can help you formulate plans relating to a future event, provided you follow the rules when you consult them. Place the tiles face down on the table and shuffle them well. Select only one tile and read the interpretation as set out below. For ordinary, immediate readings you should use only one tile but for very special purposes, two tiles may be read in conjunction.

You should not tempt fate and repeat the exercise straight away but wait several days before you try again. If the same tiles appear twice then the meaning will be intensified.

This is the most widely appreciated meaning within a set of tiles:

Blank-blank: Most unfortunate immediate and long-term outcome to your plans.

One-blank: Someone with influence who could help you.

One-one: Mostly fortunate.

Two-blank: You will not be able to manage on your own, seek help.

Two-one: Some form of security to get a loan needed.

Two-two: Partnerships should be avoided for the time being.

Three-blank: Children play an important role in immediate plans.

Three-one: Secret information could be suddenly available.

Three-two: No point in taking a gamble of any kind.

Three-three: Invitation to a celebration may not turn out well for you.

Four-blank: Unfavourable communication will arrive.

Four-one: Resources will be severely taxed trying to keep up.

Four-two: The unsuspecting could be taken for a ride.

Four-three: Domestic or family disputes possible.

Four-four: Control your diet, both food and drink.

Five-blank: A sad period, perhaps a loss of a friend.

Five-one: Unwise emotional inclinations lead to trouble.

Five-two: Could be to your advantage if near water.

Five-three: The boss may select you for a project.

Five-four: A small flutter should be result in your favour.

Five-five: A change of address is possible.

Six-blank: Keep a low profile and be careful who you trust.

Six-one: Impromptu act of kindness to another.

Six-two: Shop for new shoes and clothes.
Six-three: An unexpected journey turns out well.
Six-four: Pay bills, write letters and make those phone calls.
Six-five: A day out with those you love is advised.
Six-six: Financial gain.

❖

With games of dice or other fortune telling disciplines there are many beliefs and superstitions involved. Dice were originally knuckle-bones used in divining the future. Later they became pebbles, usually suitably endorsed with special markings which eventually evolved into modern dice as we know them today.

❖

An ancient game of chance called Five-stones once called Knucklebones was and still is a great favourite among young children but often played more by girls than boys. Like dice, they evolved along similar lines. Initially, they would have been made from carved hooves. As these would have been scarce, pebbles were rubbed and polished and cherry stones were a suitable alternative. Some exquisitely carved bones have been found set with beautiful jewels of all kind.

❖

Gambling with dice is as old as the hills and universally played. Rank did not matter, everyone gambled or played with them. However, as time went by, people began to believe in strange stories and superstitions involving them. Soon, they began to be used in fortune telling mostly just using two dice, but three are often used.

❖

The following interpretations use three dice and they are a composite from many different sources:

Three: A surprise is in store.
Four: A wish is likely to come to fruition.
Five: A new acquaintance is about to enter your life.
Six: A loss of valuable property through carelessness.

Seven: Best to keep a low profile, secrets are likely to be revealed.

Eight: Someone is trying to blame you for something they have done.

Nine: Make a wish; you ought to be very lucky in love.

Ten: An outstanding religious obligation is offered.

Eleven: An increase in personal possessions from a surprising source.

Twelve: A communication of some importance is on the way.

Thirteen: Problems ahead, possibly to do with romance.

Fourteen: A new lover is about to enter your life.

Fifteen: Keep away from troublemakers.

Sixteen: Travel is indicated.

Seventeen: Anything to with liquids is important and lucky.

Eighteen: A lucky throw implying a sudden change for the better.

These beliefs were enhanced if you were to find a single die that appeared to have been mislaid. The number showing uppermost was the key. Sometimes the dice are thrown into a pre-drawn circle. Only those that actually fall in the circle should count. If the throw is duplicated, trouble will ensue or, some say, there may be news from a long way away. One die falling and remaining on top of another implies an imminent dispute but a present of some kind is probable.

There is an old superstition that if one blows on dice before they are cast it will bring special good luck, for you are endowing them with the breath of life which in turn summons up special lucky powers. You are allowed to ask a woman companion to breathe on them for you, but not a male friend.

No real gambler will lend money to anyone. This means that if the borrower then wins with that money the lender will begin to experience a losing streak. After the sporting event, you may decide to take yourself off to have a drink at the local inn. Until very recently, if a single woman went into a bar on her own or with a (female) friend, they would have created a stir and may even have been asked to leave.

In just about all societies, cultures and religious states this largely stems from man's primitive fear of women when they are menstruating, pregnant or about to give birth. From time immemorial, man has avoided womenfolk when they are in any of these conditions.

It is at these times a woman is believed to be at her most powerful and influential. In many countries in male dominated areas men still refuse to accept a woman as an equal. In some Middle Eastern countries she is still avoided and not allowed to take part in normal social life until the demons had left her. This has given rise to the expression used by many a woman for her periods to be called the curse.

Thus, in the early part of the twentieth century when a woman decided to have a night out with the girls she and her friends were frowned on and even thought to be loose women. There was danger if anyone went too near them. Decent folk did not want them, for they were a threat to the balance of the local society and such women were feared. If they became too influential it was thought improper to entertain them unless they were properly escorted – by a man, of course. Around 150 years or so ago in England, few women ventured forth on a social call unescorted by a man – it just wasn't the thing.

She could go shopping, call on neighbours, visit a sick friend but that was it. If she tried anything else she earned a whispering criticism by the men who would create stories regarding her moral nature. Local women would have crossed her off their list of people to invite. Society was cruel in those days – and still is in many ways.

When a man enters a hostelry, a number of beliefs were attached to how matters should proceed. It was rare for a man to drink alone for, if he should become intoxicated, he was fair game for footpads. Drink was the fuel of the devil and a good way to gain a man's soul when his wits were fuddled.

The belief of drinking to the health of an absent or sick friend has its roots in early Pagan religious rites when men drank to the gods and to the dead. The gods had to be appeased regularly and the dead guided properly to their final resting place. Similarly, it was thought very unlucky not to drink at a wake or a wedding, even if one was not a drinker in the real sense.

❖

Today, non-drinkers are expected to charge their glasses for a toast with water if necessary, for not to drink at such a time was and still is an insult. One had to pay one's way and it was unlucky not to pay for a round. In more modern times a kitty would be organised for such affairs. The basis of drinking beer and wines collectively in a bar or at home has its origins in the early days when water was precious – "aqua vitae", the water of life. As time passed, certain additives and alternatives became the norm but, in all other respects, the basis of it is still water.

❖

Whatever the custom, belief or superstition in your locale may be, it all stems from when a man stopped to drink. Curiously, all other business of the day would also stop. Whether it was fighting, trading or farming, everyone was expected to stop what they were doing and join in. Combatants knew they were safe for the time being and traders realised they would not lose any advantage. Because of the way those who worked the land operated, it was sensible for all of them to stop at the same time. Thus, drinking rites and rituals may all be traced back to these times and, of course religious observations.

❖

So, it now remains to make the journey home, the day is almost over and bed beckons. But before you go more than a few steps, you realise it is raining and quite hard as well.

It is time to put up the umbrella to stay dry. This rather humble yet most prestigious symbol of modern man has a whole host of beliefs and superstitions attached to it and from a surprising source as well.

Up until quite recently, it was quite unusual to see this (seemingly) ever necessary symbol of an Englishman open and being used, even when it was raining. It has acquired the dignity of a status symbol all its own but few realise that when one is held open, it becomes a very strong symbol of leadership.

❖

The umbrella was a traditional symbol of Chinese royal dignity and used by royal princes as a protection against the Sun, yet it was never actually carried by them. Only servant attendants were allowed to be official bearers.

❖

But sometimes these umbrellas were so big they were more like canopies and they needed several men to manage them. As in all things, there was a natural pecking order.

❖

The most senior servant would supervise or be held responsible for their carriage while the royal umbrella remained closed. Another official took over when it was opened. And it is here, perhaps, that could be one answer as to why some businessmen seem so reluctant to open their umbrella – even when it is raining. It might have been construed as a loss of face then but today, after all, it is only used to keep the water off.

❖

And so you reach home once again. You must enter the house by the door you left earlier. Before you lock it, make sure you check in the mirror in case the devil hasn't entered with you.

❖

This is one of the many superstitions associated with having a mirror placed inside the front door other than the sheer practicality to check that you are properly dressed before you answer the door or go out.

Careers and Jobs

AT WORK

All occupations, jobs, pursuits and careers are littered with their fair share of superstitions. The service industry, public transport, sport or entertainment – even the armed services, are rife with their own special beliefs, irrespective of occupation or position within that activity.

The butcher, the baker and the candlestick-maker – all have their own stories, tales and ancient beliefs that they still observe for reasons no one really knows but to which almost everyone pay their respects. Some are traceable; a few are quite obvious; the rest are totally mystifying even by today's standards.

❖

For example, it has long been thought in many countries that it is ill-advised to sweep the pavements in front of the shop or store before the working day begins because you are considered to be sweeping away your potential trade for that day.

❖

Sales made before the proper opening time of the shop, especially on a Monday, the normal first day of the trading week, are said to be very fortunate indeed. The rest of the week will be a very highly profitable affair which explains why some stores open earlier than the advertised times. Change given at this transaction should be wiped or cleaned first to retain this luck.

The small businessman will prosper if he marries then starts up a new trade using his new wife's dowry money. Some folk will not launch their new company until the New Moon, the symbol of growth in every country. Few people will start a new job on a Friday or on an odd-numbered day; especially the 13th but we will deal with the mysteries of numbers more fully elsewhere.

The mid-week early closing day in Britain is now almost something of the past that even now always seemed have varied from area to area. Tuesday, ruled by the planet Mars, was chosen by some because sales people used to market their new products on this day and the buying and selling activities were quite aggressive.

Wednesday, Mercury's day, was chosen by others so they could attend to the books, buy new stock and pay their bills, all of which come under the ruler-ship of the winged messenger. It was also a favourite day for the Freemasons to hold their meetings.

Thursday is ruled by Jupiter and his domain is expansion. Much of what was believed about Tuesday holds true here as well. However, more new things come onto the market on a Thursday than almost any other day. It is worth noting here that many magazines are published on this day.

In the early days of trade and those first uneasy contacts between the nations started up, markings of some kind were needed to define ownership of goods, before and after sales. The first clumsy labelling systems to be used were coloured clay tags. Eventually, they began to use seals to make recognition even easier. The seal soon became a mark of quality, or otherwise, of course.

The best organisations flourished and their seal has now been translated into the modern corporate logo. These logos can be comprised of anything and such lucky insignias are instantly recognisable. Traditionally, it has always been thought extremely unlucky to change such signatures. If the most famous logo mark in the world, the "M" arch of MacDonald's was done away with now, the firm would suffer very heavy losses, This often happens after one company takes over another for, as one absorbs the other, losses occur which are very hard to make up. Thus, the mark, or what constitutes as a mascot for the business, is considered to be very lucky and most are protected by strict copyright laws.

❖

The most widely used are small animals or insects and jewellery but a whole host of other items can feature on the documentation or even on the tie worn by the salesmen of that company to promote their products.

❖

The handshake after an agreement has been negotiated binds the bargain and has long been the symbol of trust and honesty. However, it not that widely realised that clasped hands also make the sign of the cross. To renege on a deal after this symbolic ritual would kill off any business very quickly indeed.

❖

Even in the 21st century many deals in a whole host of business areas all over the world are still confirmed by a handshake. However, very little serious business is completed or signed up on a Friday with even fewer folk likely to start a business trip on this day.

THE BUILDING TRADE

In the construction world, the laying of the cornerstone is treated with the utmost respect. Superstition says that if Satan does not try to take the building for himself, one of the many Earth gods will do so.

Centuries ago, human and animal sacrifices were made and the body would have been laid under one corner of the building – a common practice in Northern Europe. The Celts were among the many who insisted on these sacrifices being made. Such activities were thought to have given rise to theory of the haunted house and, in a few houses a circle would be drawn out and a knife put in it to show that it or the owner had the protection of the local witch.

These days a scroll or any other certificate tends to make do. Even today, when modern ceremonies take place, it was and often still is preferred by the men that no women should attend, especially an unmarried one. In some areas it was thought that if she were engaged to be married her wedding might be delayed for some reason. It was also possible that it might not take place at all. Either way, if a woman were to be present at such a time, any later construction work could suffer many delays.

Virgins were always considered to make the best human sacrifices to appease the spirits because it was believed they brought good luck all round, except to themselves. In these more enlightened times, a prominent or well-known business person is given the honour of laying a cornerstone. It is usually someone who holds a recognised office in the trade, or a Freemason, or both!

BAKERS

Bakers still bake thirteen loaves to a dozen for in medieval times tax collectors were ruthless if the bread they examined was underweight. Only one baker should handle the oven at a time, otherwise they will quarrel. In this day and age, some bakers still refuse to slice fresh bread for it has always been felt unlucky to cut one loaf while another is baking.

In Wales, if a split appears along the top of a loaf after it has been baked, it signals bad luck for whoever eats the first or last slice. In olden times and even these days in a few areas it may be withdrawn from sale. Many country bakers still make the sign of the cross as they put their dough into the oven to protect the bake.

WINDOW CLEANERS

The window cleaner is reputed to dislike having to work where another of their number has fallen. Nevertheless, they are still seen to set up their equipment in much the same way and place because they also believe that a change of routine can cause a change of luck.

FLORISTS

Some flower sellers will not mix red and white flowers together if they know they are for a sick person, for these two colours are recognised as the colours of poor health. One should wrap them separately for good luck and or a speedy recovery. Other florists dislike mixing out-of-season blossoms with fresh flowers and nor will they recommend you to display white flowers in a house, for that is said to signal death or disease.

HAIR DRESSERS AND BARBERS

In some quarters it thought unwise and unlucky to cut hair on Tuesdays and Saturdays. Tuesday is ruled by Mars, the God of War and a cut could prove to be fatal. Saturday is ruled by Saturn and it is thought that a haircut on this day could reduce life by seven months. Thursday is ruled by Jupiter the planet of expansion and presages good luck.

Do not give anyone scissors on this day as a gift to a friend or a hairdresser or that association will come to an abrupt end. Always bury cut hair or wrap it and bury it deep in a garden, for that will help create increased growth. Remove a single grey hair (at any age) and eight more will grow in its place.

MILLINERS AND TAILORS

The fashion trade has its share of strange beliefs. Very few milliners, or tailors for that matter, will start a new hat or garment on a Friday for it will bring the eventual wearer bad luck unless, of course it can be finished on the same day. It is very unlucky to lose your thimble on a Saturday. If you drop a needle and it sticks in the floor, it is a good omen.

◈

You must never lend or give a pin to anyone; you should make them take it if they ask and they should not verbally thank you. This belief probably stems from when pins were so rare and expensive, especially in the 15th century when they could only (or should only) have been sold on the first two days of January. It is known that women would save for their "pin-money" each year because they were such useful things to have.

◈

This ancient doggerel reflects the belief: "See a pin and pick it up, and all that day you'll have good luck. See a pin and let it lay, you'll have misfortune all that day."

◈

People in the clothing industry dislike making adjustments to anything while it is being worn. Many believe it will drive the wearer mad but, if any alterations are necessary, many hold a small piece of thread in between their teeth to offset this, but no one can say why.

◈

If scissors fall to the ground you should tread on them before picking them up. Never cross two pairs of scissors because it is said that it will start an argument. Never put scissors down in an open position for they make the sign of the cross. Superstition says this will bring bad luck for whoever leaves them that way.

It is lucky to put clothing on inside out when you dress first thing in the morning. One is expected to leave the item as it is for the whole day or you will change that luck.

❖

In some African countries the dead are deliberately dressed with their clothes on inside out to fool the devil or his minions who might be on the lookout for new souls. It is said that the devil knows what the person looked like while he or she was alive but he would not recognise them dressed in such a way.

❖

Women often wear a triangular shaped headscarf shaped from a piece of square material and that is considered very lucky. Women are also expected to cover their head when in church and this is one way they are likely to do it. However, they are supposed to use the square material as it stands. This is quite a popular belief in the southern USA states and in South American countries generally. It is believed the triangular shape represents the cross and, therefore, protects the women.

❖

The square is a symbol of power and is why it is so often seen in male formal or religious wear. Much of the insignia worn by priests reflects these ancient, originally Pagan, beliefs.

SHOES

Shoes have a long and distinctive treasury of unusual superstitions and beliefs associated with them. The Chinese thought of them as a sex symbol and women were not allowed to show their feet, shod or otherwise, in polite society. Among ancient Assyrians, Egyptians and Hebrews shoes or, to be more precise, sandals, were exchanged as a symbol of possession in much the same way a modern deal is confirmed by a handshake. It was unlucky to renege after the exchange of footwear.

Many warriors of those times wore only one sandal in battles but there are no clear-cut reasons for this. Certain religious practices of the time required one foot to be bare and one covered and this could be a reflection of these beliefs.

❖

In Anglo-Saxon times the father of a bride would present his future son-in-law with a pair of her shoes to symbolise and show how binding the agreement was regarded. In Norway it is still believed that when a family come together on special occasions they must place their shoes in a line to signify they will do their best to keep the peace between them in the following weeks and months.

❖

High heels have always been revered for many ancient kings wore them to exaggerate their height to emphasise their importance. This practice may have found its way into Celtic belief where their royalty wore only red shoes to show their rank. No one else was allowed to do so on pain of death. In many ways, the belief that shoes have special properties has found its way into the ritual of either throwing or tying them to the car or carriage of newly-weds for luck. Sailors often have shoes thrown at them when they set sail, for luck.

❖

In parts of old Ireland, newly elected local officials would have shoes thrown over their heads to bring them good fortune. It is said that when Queen Victoria first entered her beloved Balmoral, the staff threw shoes over her.

❖

When dressing first thing in the morning, you must always put your right shoe on first or the devil had a fair chance for claiming you later in the day. In various sporting arenas this particular belief is so strongly followed that some players have been known to not play if they make this mistake.

AT PLAY

GOLF

Many golfers will not start a round at 1 o'clock, the thirteenth hour of the day. Many prefer to play with a ball with an odd number on it which has to be visible to the player as he strikes it. Other golfers will take an old club around with them as a symbol of luck and they will not clean a ball if things are going their way.

FOOTBALL

Football is ridden with its own set of really strange superstitions. Club administrators feel it almost essential to have some kind of mascot. Often, a young boy or girl or an animal is dressed up for the occasion. This practice has its origins in the dim and distant past.

◈

The mascot of today is a modern representation of the old sacrifice to be offered before those important gatherings of the past. In those days, as the Church struggled to establish itself, the practice was changed to a symbolic offering and the mascot took its place.

CRICKET

Cricket, as we have come to know it, came into being about the turn of the 17th century and is a long cry from the game first played in the county of Surrey called "creag" in 1300 or "cricket" in the 1590's. Until very recently, both teams had to play in subdued whites and under very strict rules.

◈

It was a game for gentleman but there are still a few superstitions found even here. Dressing rituals are observed; the right leg-pad to be put on before the left, the right glove donned first and a cap must be worn. If the player walks to the wicket and discovers he has put the wrong pad on the wrong leg he must wait to bat last for he believes he will not score or be responsible for someone else not scoring or that he will be run out.

❖

In local games such beliefs are very strictly believed. One must always acknowledge both umpires and the opposing captain on his way in to bat. Players of both sides must not show displeasure when he is out. To reach 111 is thought unlucky, for it looks like three wickets without the bails. This is called a "Nelson".

❖

One now retired umpire always stood on one leg until the player moved on to a higher score. It is said that bowlers who miss their stride as they run up to bowl will ask or even insist in a few cases to be taken off, for they feel that their luck has changed to the other side.

❖

Before a match, two or more players of the same team must not wash their hands in the same water or they will not score. This superstition spread to football and other games for a long while.

ANGLING

Angling is rife with all manner of beliefs. Few will sit on an upturned bucket for they will have spilled their luck. In Scotland and Kent it is extremely unlucky to hold a rod with the left hand and cast with the right (what do left-handed people do?). If you see an earwig on the way to the river you should take it with you for good luck. One should not put the catch net into the water before the first fish is caught or you may not catch anything.

SEA-FISHING

Sea-fishermen do not like setting out on a Friday, nor will they like a woman or a priest on board. If they cut themselves by accident they will press a lugworm over the wound then throw it into the water while they let their hand dangle in the sea. The worm removes the evil and the sea will clean the wound.

It is believed by many European fishermen that to catch a female fish first means a good haul, while a male brings poor results. At such times this first fish should be nailed to the mast as an appeasement to the God of the Fish. Do not count your haul or no more will be caught in that sailing. In parts of coastal Northern England it was and still is thought to be unlucky to burn fish bones. They should be given to gardeners who live nearby who will grind them up and use them as fertiliser.

HORSE RACING

In horseracing circles there is a wealth of different beliefs coloured by country and area. You must never change the name of a horse or wish it good luck before a race. Jockeys will use "lucky" colours. They must never put their boots on a clean floor or on a table either.

In Northern Europe many trainers and even a few owners carry frog bones on them. An extremely old traditional magical recipe for powdered frog's bones with a few other similar ingredients exists for which, among other things, it is thought can be made up to help master horses.

Spotted horses, those with splashes of colour or, depending on where you live, pure white horses are all thought to be lucky. In Devon, a horse with four white feet is avoided because the locals maintain they are unlucky. If you should meet up with such a horse, make the sign of the cross in the ground or keep two fingers crossed until you meet with a dog.

The Norse God Odin was believed to have raced on a dapple grey (although some say it had eight legs) which accounts for why so many people feel this colour horse is lucky. In the UK, and some continental countries, if a jockey drops his whip before the race he will not win.

❖

After the advent of photography in the 19th century, people began to believe that if a photograph was taken of the jockey and his mount prior to a race, they would lose. With the development of television, this superstition has had to go by the board.

❖

The expression "go by the board" is a very old nautical term meaning lost overboard or to be so has long been forgotten.

❖

A horse's mane must never be seen to have a tangle in it because in the north of England this is known as a hag-knot and the horse could belong to a local witch. A hair or two from a horse's mane in this state was greatly treasured by young village girls. They would weave them into their own locks to help them dream of their future lover.

THE ENTERTAINMENT WORLD

It is very well known in and out of the entertainment world how superstitious an actor or an actress can be. When rehearsals go too well some of them have been known to become quite upset and then they deliberately fail to speak their final lines or say them properly so that they do not get everything right before the real event takes place.

This superstition has its roots in Buddhist and Hindu beliefs that man can never be perfect in this life. Man should always be in a constant state of striving to become perfect but must never be actually so. Actors believe to be perfect is to be dead. He or she will display public modesty when praised while inwardly they will be brimming over with pleasure.

ACTORS

One should never wish an actor good luck or they will say something along the lines of "Break a leg" as a form of admonition. Mostly, people tend to say "Break a leg" as a matter of course these days. Actors and actresses prefer not to look at the audience from between the curtains because they may inadvertently look at them from the wrong or unlucky side. They will use a special flap built into the right curtain so that they can never make that mistake.

❖

Macbeth, perhaps more widely appreciated as "The Scottish Play" by the acting profession has many superstitions associated with it. Mostly, it is because the Witches' song and dance scene is claimed to have the power of working evil and the probable cause for many accidents involving those who take part.

❖

For as long as this scene remains on the stage and is not performed off-stage or elsewhere, its bad luck is quite unable to spread to other folk or areas. In its long history, there have been many reported incidents such as breakages, losses, fires and other accidents.

❖

There has been one death at least – that of Lilian Baylis at the Old Vic in London. This lady had a heart attack on November 25th 1937, the day before the play was set to open. If ever a play had superstition attached to it, then Macbeth takes centre-stage.

❖

To see butterflies fluttering across a live stage is thought to be very lucky indeed. Butterflies are thought to carry the souls of the dearly departed and to see one means that someone has managed to return to encourage your endeavours.

No one must whistle in a theatre, especially a woman. This is thought to be a way of conjuring up evil spirits who live in the wind. Whistling is copying the wind. People who make this mistake are made to leave the room they are in and turn round three times in a sun-wise direction. After this they may re-enter the room. Others say that whoever whistles in the dressing room could cause someone, not necessarily the whistler, to be out of work. If a woman is the whistler, it is doubly bad luck.

One must not open any first-night good-luck telegrams until the first performance is over. Knitting is frowned upon because any knots made on a stage are very unlucky. If there is a call for knitting it should be simulated to offset ill fortune. Green has always been considered bad luck but colours and their charms or otherwise will vary from theatre to theatre, from town to town and country to country.

THEATRES AND STUDIOS

Theatre employees have their fair share of activities to avoid. They must note the apparent age of the first person to buy a ticket at the box-office. If young, the show will not run for long, but if it is an older person, then the play should have a long and profitable run. Women should not tip theatre attendants, who may well refuse to accept it anyway.

Quite a few of the beliefs and superstitions found in the theatre have been carried over to film and television studios. There are very few actors, or directors for that matter, who are keen to work on more than thirteen takes of any scene. They are inclined to stop and try again at another time or another date.

A missing button, a tear or rip in a stage garment will put some actors in an absolute frenzy until it is rectified; it must be replaced while he or she is still wearing it. Practical jokes are never really encouraged and one must never blow up a paper bag and burst it in a film or TV studio.

Pointing with the index finger of the right hand on stage is thought to bring bad luck because this is the poison finger. In Europe it is well known as the "witches" finger, the one with which they used to "throw" their poison.

PANTOMIME

In pantomime, the story of Cinderella is favoured by performers for it brings good luck, much the same as the story it depicts but "Babes in the Wood" and "Robin Hood" are thought very unlucky.

THE BALLET

Ballet and opera people have their share of beliefs and superstitions, mostly along the same lines as the ordinary theatre folk but with a few extras thrown in for good measure.

❖

Ballerinas have specialised ways of wishing other performers good luck which varies from company to company. They all tend to have lucky hair brushes with which they do their hair, favoured make-up brushes and powder puffs to be used in the right order each time they prepare for a performance and they must never vary this routine.

❖

In both the ballet or in musicals, members of the chorus may well keep a heel of an old dancing shoe about them for good luck – many swear by it.

THE OPERA

Singers hold with many of the beliefs associated with the play Macbeth and carry them over in the operatic version. Elsewhere, in other operas some arias are regarded lucky or otherwise. "Tosti's Farewell" may not be sung anywhere in a theatre save during a proper performance.

In the orchestra pit, there are many musicians who dislike being paid before a performance and there are players who refuse to accept their pay until afterwards. Many musicians will not carry or store an instrument they cannot play – it is very bad luck. This has connections with the Church when only musicians were allowed in a special part of a church on ceremonial occasions.

Peacock feathers tend to be disliked by performers almost everywhere. This is whether they are worn as a prop by the actors or if members of the audience wear them. Neither do they welcome fresh flowers. This is why no matter how good they may look, false ones must always be used. However, a bouquet presented at the end of the performance is allowed.

First Night should not take place on a Friday. Many actors and actresses on stage or in a film or TV studio prefer not to allow three spotlights to follow them about on the stage.

Dancers or singers dislike wearing yellow, for this was used for dressing the devil minion's when they were not dressed in the traditional red normally associated with Satan.

Green, of course, no one likes because it is attributed to the little people and those who dare to wear anything green may be carried away by them. However, away from the theatre it is considered more of a lucky colour because it is associated with new growth and the spirits of the plant world.

In Northern Europe it is thought lucky to place greenery over doorways to symbolise good luck and help keep away witches and demons – but never over a theatre entrance or exit.

THE CIRCUS

In the circus many of the superstitions to do with performing in public will be found. Some beliefs where colours are concerned are thought to be over exaggerated. Red is dangerous because it is regarded as the colour of the devil. Very few acrobats or tightrope walkers would dare to even think about wearing it. Black of course is the colour of death and avoided like the plague by everyone. But in the orient, where white is the colour associated with death and mourning, black is quite acceptable.

❖

Once again, it depends on the area, but a black cat seen in or near the circus could cause pandemonium. Some people dread the sight of one anywhere while others do not care a great deal either way. Traditionally, the black cat is thought to be a descendant of Bast, the cat worshipped by the Egyptians.

❖

To see one meant the Goddess Hathor had despatched a messenger in this shape to bring you into her presence. Whether this was a good thing or a bad thing depends much on your belief in the luck of cat cults.

The Services

THE NAVY

The armed services are known to have their fair share of superstitions, especially the senior service. Navy men all over the world dislike the idea of a thief on board. The loss of personal belongings is one thing but many feel that even the ship loses some of its luck when someone is found stealing.

❖

For countless years and even today, the vast majority of sailors of all ranks and jobs dislike and will try to avoid sailing in a ship with a name that ends with the letter "A".

❖

In Wales, in medieval times it was believed by sailors that a few sips of seawater taken daily would enhance longevity. Many coastal dwellers still follow the custom of hanging dried seaweed inside the house. Its presence is not only thought to drive away evil spirits it is also thought to stop the house catching fire.

❖

Seaweed hung in the porch is for a different reason for it is widely thought to help you know the weather. If it is going to be dry and sunny, it shrivels up. If rain is on the way it will swell up and feel moist to the touch.

❖

Sailors are afraid of and will not ill-treat seagulls for they believe each one is the spirit of a drowned shipmate. To kill a gull means evil will always follow shortly after. When these birds fly inland there is bad weather at sea, for fish dive too deeply at such times and the birds cannot reach them.

❖

So, the birds come inland for their food but if a seagull is seen to sit on your roof there may be sickness and or an impending death in the family. Similarly, if a gull should land on a ship, tragedy will not be far away for at least one of the crew.

❖

Swallows that fly across the sea are believed by sailors to carry little bits of twig or wood with them from their native land with which they will build their new nest. To find and keep such a twig suggests that the sailor might live and eventually die in that country.

THE AIR FORCE

Air Force pilots frequently carry small charms to offset bad luck and many of these often involve little pieces of wood. However, to "touch wood" as such, means that these people must actually touch a piece of proper wood and not just a chair or table.

❖

During WWII many pilots would empty their pockets on return from a sortie of any kind. This was meant as a symbol not unlike a sacrificial offering for their safe return. American pilots in particular would uncross any unused seat belts before they took off to appease the unknown spirits of the air.

❖

In civil airlines even in this 21st century there is a universal dislike of passengers who bring flowers on board a plane, especially red and white ones for these are considered to be the traditional symbols of life and death as well as that of doctors and barbers, who often used to act as doctors.

There are a few pilots who dislike having to fly if the previous night the Full Moon had streaks of clouds in straight lines floating across the front. In Europe, at the beginning of flight in the last century, it was felt these lines represented the spirits of those who passed on but who had come back to collect more souls for the next day. This is much in line with many of the old sailor's beliefs from the Pacific area.

Flight in general terms has not yet come of age to allow superstition, beliefs, and other similar thoughts to take proper root. But we do know that even the astronauts had lucky charms and mascots of all kinds with them on their early space flights. Astronauts who have flown on recent space flights have admitted that one or two of them have carried a special charm or two, just in case!

Many of these old superstitions I have just outlined have their origins in the lore of the ancient seafarer and old land traveller. Links among many of these now widespread ideas are to be found in the old writings of countries as far apart as China, India, Egypt and the north European states.

THE ARMY

In the British army, many beliefs and superstitions found in the much older regiments are often repeated in some of the other divisions of the North American army. However, with these people, some of the beliefs also stem from faraway places like France, Germany, and Holland. People from the Nordic communities brought their fair share of superstitions with them, as did the seafarers of Italy, Portugal, Greece and other lands in the near vicinity.

Many of these old stories have found their way out of the army and into civilian life. However, perhaps none is more widely spoken of and believed in than the "three on one match" story. This has been traced to several dates in the middle of the 20th century but, for the most part, it has its roots in and dates more properly from the 1914-1918 war.

Soldiers everywhere have an intense dislike of allowing three cigarettes to be lit from the same match. Huddling together in the trenches, those who wanted a quick smoke tended to light their cigarettes from one match mostly to keep the glow to a minimum.

Two could light up fairly quickly but it was known and accepted that a sharp-eyed marksman from the other side would have time to take aim and fire by the time the third man took his light. Thus, this third man would probably be wounded or killed in the act. It is not widely known but the reason it did not happen much in World War II was because there was a shortage of matches.

❖

Similar stories date from very many early civilisations. When a local chief died, it became time for the ritual of all tribal fires except his to be put out. Priests would then re-light them all three at a time, each with a stick from the late chief's fire for they were thought to retain his spirit – but which stick did so no one could be sure.

❖

At about the turn of the 10th century the Church took on this role which is seen today in the way priests may light only three candles from one taper at a time. It became a belief that for anyone other than an ordained priest to do this would be a very unlucky thing to do. This belief is now very widespread in many countries all over the world.

❖

Some old soldiers who come from the north of England have been known to carry little lumps of coal as a protective charm against being wounded. In a few very rare cases, sailors do this to ensure they will return.

❖

Soldiers from central European areas dislike hearing birds sing before a battle for they think it portends massive casualties for both sides. If any soldier, especially a commander, misses his step and stumbles before a battle it is a terrible omen, for it is thought he will not return.

It is considered extremely unlucky to talk about religious or political subjects before a battle because nerves, already a little frayed, can cause tempers to rise and quarrels begin among soldiers on the same side which was hardly a helpful situation.

❖

The "V" sign is considered as rather lucky to be found on an amulet in Belgium and Holland. This follows on from similar thinking in the old Egyptian, Greek and Roman empires. It was not a new gesture introduced by Sir Winston Churchill in World War II, as many think; it was meant as a sign of good luck.

If you look carefully you will note that Churchill holds his hand up face on to the viewer: The much misunderstood version which is also thought to be extremely rude is where the hand is held up with the back of the hand being shown to the viewer.

Both versions of the "V" sign are used not just by fighting men in the navy, the air force and the army, but also by civilians of either sex the world over. Originally, it dates back to Egyptian pre-history when Horus the God was thrown into the pit of darkness by Set the Evil. Horus' father, the great God Osiris, helped his son escape up a ladder.

❖

Horus then used it to help others escape using the strength in his first two fingers and from then on two upraised fingers facing you has always meant encouragement while the same two fingers in reverse or pointing downward implied derision.

❖

In the Middle Ages this same sign was made during the wars against the French by English bowmen who had escaped their captivity. To make sure captured archers would never fire a bow again, the French would amputate the two middle fingers and then, eventually, let them go in deals for the exchange of prisoners.

However, many of these soldiers escaped and returned to their own lines under their own steam. Later, in battle, they would make the "V" sign to the enemy by holding aloft their first and fourth fingers palm side away from the enemy, then all the fingers would be raised. Such a gesture enraged the enemy and, it was hoped, made them unable to think clearly. This is now an accepted belief or superstition for enemies to make these gestures to annoy the other side, however large or small the dispute.

THE SALUTE

The salute should always be made with the right hand, for left-handed folk are mistrusted in many places all over the world. The Latin word for left is "sinister" and left-handers are still thought sinister or unlucky people to know no matter what country you may be in.

The origin of the salute goes back over many years. It is easy to understand why so many infamous drill sergeants have insisted that it is correctly made because if this original greeting were ever improperly carried out it could have meant death.

To greet another person with the open hand is a time-honoured salutation indicating a friendly intention. To hold the head and body erect is a reminder that we are free men. The hand gesture to the head goes back to when knights in full armour opened their visor to allow each to see the face of the other. The empty hand and the open visor were a sign of friendliness and that neither need fear the other.

The officers' salute with a sword is a reminder of when knights kissed the sword before a fight. At the first recover position, that is, when the officer pulls the sword toward himself, he is unable to engage in a fight. When he lowers the sword it is a symbol of trust because when it is in this position he cannot attack without giving plenty of warning.

The old custom of holding a weapon so that it cannot be used is more or less universal but tailored to the country and the tradition where it is used. It has always been widely believed that any error is an insult but reaction varies with prevailing circumstances. It is, therefore, extremely unlucky to make a mistake with a salute.

THE CIVILIAN SERVICES

THE POLICE

The police service, and criminals for that matter, each have wide ranging beliefs and superstitions that are fairly similar in their make-up and origins. They may differ very slightly from country to country but they are fairly easy to trace, irrespective of which side the character may be involved.

Before we delve into them, it is worth noting that about 70 years ago Britain still had the Witchcraft Act on the Statute Book. It was eventually repealed in 1951, but not before a couple of minor trials that involved an astrologer and a medium who were tried under the Act just prior to it being taken off.

❖

In those days most criminals had a great respect for their local bobby. In the late 1940's I still recall a police constable who, on finding a man clearly in breach of the law (a bookie's "runner" caught totally red-handed) told him to report to the local police station about thirty minutes later. He was told not to go home or get rid of any evidence he may have had on him.

❖

The runner followed his instructions to the letter and duly reported at the station and waited for the officer to arrive, such was his respect. He was charged and appeared in the magistrate's court the following day where he pleaded guilty and then agreed the facts of the "arrest".

The magistrate told him he was a lucky man for if he had not done as he had been asked he would have gone to prison for 28 days. He was fined ten shillings. In our present climate, such a thing is unthinkable but, in those days, people on the wrong side of the law respected the opposition born out of the superstitious beliefs of yesteryear.

This is a far cry from medieval times when felons were dealt with such brutality. Hanging offences were rife and, as executions almost always took place on a Friday, the day became synonymous with bad luck, certainly for the criminal. For a long time in the United States, Friday was known as Hangman's Day.

❖

An ancient Saxon manuscript claims that anyone who was born on a Friday was "an accursed of men ...and shall be a thief all his life", and if that day is also the 13th he really was considered to be a most unlucky soul.

❖

Until quite recently, very little crime was committed on a Friday for, if caught, suspects were kept locked up until the following Monday and only then would they be brought before a magistrate.

❖

Police officers did not like Fridays either. To find a dead body or begin a murder investigation was very unlucky for it was thought that the soul of such a crime victim lingered behind and might attach itself to anyone nearby. This would continue until the matter was fully resolved or until the dead person's correct life span came due. The connection with the Crucifixion is very strong in this belief.

❖

It has also long been believed for many years that the image of the killer is imprinted in the eyes of the victim. Further, anyone who found a murdered body was also thought to be equally unlucky, for he or she could "see" who did it and they could be marked as the next victim by the killer.

❖

Monday has never been the most popular of days for anyone, no matter what their calling. And, coming as it does after the usual hedonistic weekend most folk seem to enjoy, tempers are often a trifle more frayed then normal. Magistrates are not exempt, and their decisions were and still are a tad likely to have a trifle more bile involved than usual.

❖

The criminal element did not like Mondays either, for it is a tradition that one should never ask for a favour on a Monday as it will not be granted. Any "deals" a suspect might want to make were doomed before they asked. In many rural areas in the south of England it was widely believed that thieves could steal and get away with it provided they carried the heart of a dead toad with them.

❖

In the United States, gamblers, bank robbers and many ordinary citizens have an intense dislike of the two-dollar bill for a variety of reasons.

❖

To alleviate the belief, anyone who gets one gambling, stealing or in their change must tear a corner off. This offsets the bad luck. This counter-magic is fine until the fifth person gets one with all four corners missing. Apparently, many people will simply tear the note up and throw it away.

❖

The two-dollar note is associated with the "deuce", the lowest number in a pack of cards. The word "deuce" is believed to be a corruption of the word "devil" and therefore naturally unlucky. In some American states it is felt that if pregnant women get a two-dollar bill they will give birth to twins!

❖

In the middle of the 19th century, the two-dollar note was used to bribe voters and it was often used by "con-artists" in their scams in the early 1900's. It would be folded in half and put inside a wad of other notes. When a wad of money is "fanned" through quickly it can then look like a twenty-dollar bill.

THE AMBULANCE SERVICE

There are no hard and fast superstitions directly attributable to this service but there are a number of widespread beliefs. For example, there has almost always been an aversion held by some people, especially in North Country areas that to see an ambulance was regarded as being quite unlucky. To avert this one was advised to "pinch your nose or hold your breath (?) until you see a black or brown dog". There was a simple little dirge to go with this:

"Touch your nose
Touch your toes
Never go in one of those
Until you see a dog."

❖

It is well known within the service that ambulance crews dislike having to work on the night of a Full Moon because they seem to spend much of their time dealing with people who appear to be affected at such times.

❖

Many people become involved in violent incidents or attempt or succeed in acts of suicide. At such times, these unfortunate people do not always care whom they unwittingly involve. Those who throw themselves off a bridge or under a train create much more harm for others, for it is the ambulance service that has to deal with these innocent bystanders as well as clear up after the event.

❖

Road traffic accidents can peak at this time as well as other so-called "silly" moments when people get themselves in some fairly daft situations. A few of these can be screamingly funny, while others are terrible tragedies that could have easily been averted.

Occasionally, Friday 13th has similar incidents with which the ambulance crews have to deal. Of late, the weekend evenings have become quite busy with many young people especially tending to either drink too much or indulge in drug taking. It is said that these nights have now become the busiest times of ambulance crews. In these modern times, there are far too many attacks on crew members and their vehicles.

THE FIRE SERVICE

Along with their ambulance colleagues, the fire service staffs have no real serious beliefs or superstitions directly attributable to them. However, in the old days at the turn of the 20th century there were a number of thoughts that took precedence over rational thinking. The fire service people also prefer not to have to turn out at Full Moon for they too experience their fair share of dealing with people affected at these times.

Many years ago and at least up to the turn of the 20th century, many of the UK fire stations had a horseshoe hung over the main entrance. The service used to be horse-drawn and many of the old horse, blacksmith and related superstitions abounded.

Today, in the early 21st century, there is an intense dislike of thunderstorms, for they, in turn, affect modern security systems that seem to be set off rather easily at such times. However, this is a largely practical consideration rather than an esoteric affair although, with time, it could grow into one. Remember that this is one way the old beliefs could have started.

Many modern fire fighters tend to join up when they leave the armed services and some of the older naval thinking and beliefs still hold sway. The fire service duty spells are still called watches and many navy beliefs regarding ladders, ladies and knots have been carried over but it must be stressed, only by a few individuals.

However, and in fairness, both the ambulance and fire services staff are so highly trained for their work that there is very little time for traditional beliefs. There is no place for them to be superstitious at such moments and I am happy to set the record straight for them.

Colours, Names and Numbers

COLOURS

Throughout history, colours and the many beliefs and superstitions associated with them have always been prominent, irrespective of any individual nations' beliefs, race and creeds. In some cases, what holds good for one country is completely opposite for another. Quite a few countries tend to reveal their preference for a particular colour in the design of their flag.

Their other public or national emblem, like the animal, flower, tree or other plant may also reflect this. In all those other life forms, like the animal or the insect world, colour plays such a very strong part that it is hardly surprising there are so many divergent beliefs. In fact, so much so, we know from practical experiments that the animal kingdom itself is very much aware of colour.

Originally, colours were associated with the then known seven planets while they, in turn, signified diverse representations but we are only interested with the colour interpretations here.

❖

The Sun, the Giver of Life, is golden yellow, and represents cheerfulness, intelligence, warmth and prosperity. The Moon, the Lady of the Night is white and indicates purity, understanding, sympathy and reserve. Mercury, the Messenger of the Gods, is silver-grey suggesting neither one thing nor another, a true independent, and a diplomat. The Goddess of Love, Venus, has the symbolic colour of green, meaning humanity, healing, growth and re-birth.

❖

Mars, the God of War's colour is red, and indicates energy, motivation, aggression and leadership while the colour of Jupiter is usually held to be purple or violet and implies aspiration and ambition along with power and authority. Saturn's colour is traditionally indigo or black from which we discern service, wisdom, respectability and duty.

❖

The modern and recently discovered (or re-discovered) heavenly bodies, Uranus, Neptune and Pluto have each been assigned colours and they deserve a mention here.

❖

Uranus' colours are a mixture of dark blue to azure and reflect the change, originality, naturalness and boldness of people born under its influence. The planet Neptune's colour is mauve or lavender, suggesting intuition and insight, vision and patience. Pluto, it is suggested, has domain over dark red or deep crimson, colours to reflect the depth and intensity of the forces of passion.

❖

Each of these colour associations fit in perfectly with the beliefs of the ancients and may well account for many of the superstitions handed down to us today. Therefore, with these modern meanings in mind, it should now become much easier to understand how these ancient beliefs and superstitions might have originated.

❖

Black has always been associated with the night and its dark forces but elsewhere it is also credited with restorative and curative powers for, during darkness, Nature is concerned with repairs. Man sleeps at night, in the dark, away from the light, to rest, restore his strength and to help maintain his physical well-being. Black, therefore, is a welcome colour, preferably at night but during daylight hours, anything black is not always that agreeable.

❖

The black cat is considered unlucky in most places especially if one should cross your path in daylight hours. The black cat is considered to be the familiar, or the companion of witches. Witches have always held to be evil, but nothing could be further from the truth.

❖

The witch or Wicca woman was a wise old woman who usually lived on her own with only a cat for company. They wore black because that material was more readily available. It was certainly a lot cheaper and much more in line with their reduced circumstances. It is also worth noting that the majority of these ladies were largely widows who tended to wear black as a matter of course anyway.

Sooner or later, nearly everybody would have paid a visit to one of these wise old ones for a cure or instructions on how to handle ill-health or whatever. These old women always had a wide knowledge and understanding of the value of herbs and natural medicines.

This information would have been handed down by word of mouth from mother to daughter in their earlier years and so on. When illness struck, one didn't go off to the surgery for a consultation with the doctor because there weren't any! The only real help one was likely to get was from one of the wise old women and then only if you had one who lived locally. As a rule, her cures helped ailments but the locals tended to forget that because of their beliefs.

When you begin to research how these cures were interpreted by laymen in those days, the art of creative thinking and, much later on, gifted and imaginative writing was carried to a very high degree – hence the superstitions of today.

Trying to get to the origins of some of these ideas has been quite a task. If the tail of a black cat is rubbed over a sty, a small inflammation that occasionally occurs on the eyelid, or when a piece of wool from the tail of a black sheep is placed on an afflicted ear, such ills will be eased and eventually cured. In rural parts of Europe and Northern England, when a shepherd died a tuft of wool from the tail of a black lamb or sheep was put into his hands. This was to let God know he could not leave his flock to go to church and that He would forgive him for not attending church.

❖

A black horse has always been thought to be able to see in the dark and many gypsies swear it has second sight. A ring or bangle made from a discarded horseshoe of a black horse is considered very lucky and even more so if it was made on a Friday.

❖

Elsewhere, a horse-brass from a team of black horses would be kept in the living room over the mantle-piece to keep away the devil himself. A farmer would always keep these brasses highly polished for the brightness would reflect the light to keep his satanic majesty at bay.

❖

In parts of India, shopkeepers will not sell black or white goods after nightfall. In the Western Hemisphere, black is the colour of death and mourning, while white is the choice in many Eastern countries. A black moth seen in a house portends a death in the family. In Europe and the United States it is the custom to wear black as the symbol of mourning while in China and Japan it is their belief to wear white. In other countries, different colours are worn. In ancient Syria they wear violet, but in Buddhist countries they don yellow or saffron robes. In ancient Persia they used to wear blue.

❖

Graphologists have always asserted that people who write with black ink need to be clearly understood at all times. Such writers are usually most assertive in their overall approach and behaviour toward other folk.

In many centuries, blue has always been believed to be the colour of life. In fact, almost everywhere this is held to be true. Nevertheless, there are a few, very few, exceptions. The colour blue protects against witches for most ordinary people believe it to be the colour of heaven. For much the same reason Egyptian Pharaohs wore blue except that for these people there was also an astrological reason behind this. A "Blue Moon" is said to be the 13th moon of the year. Here in the UK, they occasionally appear and it is said that it is very lucky to see one.

This is also one reason why brides wear "something blue" for it is the colour of the Moon, the traditional protector of all unmarried women. Blue-eyed people are said to have magical powers and sapphires have always been thought to be the luckiest of gems. People who write with blue ink are alleged to be outgoing and sympathetic, loyal friends and good workers. Pale blue suggests an artistic and creative nature, while dark blue implies someone who does well in a position of authority and responsibility.

❖

Green is the symbol of growth and re-birth and the colour figures quite strongly in fertility rites and rituals all over the world. However, many people feel it is unlucky to wear green. "Wear green and your family will soon wear black" is an old doggerel that dates back a long time, probably to the Middle Ages. This was a time when the colour green was associated with poison and bad luck.

This is not so in Ireland where green is considered very lucky and we all know about the luck of the Irish. People who write with green ink tend to be emotionally dependent; they do not like to be one of a crowd. Young people, particularly the girls, will often use this ink especially after a romance breaks up.

❖

Brown has a diverse history in the beliefs of men. On the one hand it has long been associated with religious beliefs, when a monk's habit was almost always of a brown shade. While on the other hand, there are still some country folk who think brown connects more with the soil of the cemetery and avoid it like the plague. Japanese folk have an intense fear of a brown or ginger cat (except for those who belong to the cat cults) and think they always bring very bad luck, in much the same we in the West dislike black cats. People who use brown ink to write with like to think that they are safe and sure in all they do, for there is a strong need to feel secure at all times.

❖

Red has always been believed to bring wealth and power. Traditionally, this was the colour magicians were supposed to have used to write out their secret formulas, especially in Europe and the Middle Eastern countries. Red amulets and precious stones are used by some people in the borderline countries near and/or between the East and the West to protect from danger during storms.

❖

For years, scarlet coloured cloths were used to staunch the blood-flow of those who fell in battle. In England, physicians would wear red to show their profession and in almost every country in the world, red has been used as a cure or preventative for a wide ranging number of ills.

❖

In most fighting areas, red is worn by military medical personnel so that the opposition forces do not accidentally fire upon a hospital or the small places where the injured and sick are being treated. Note that we in the Western world use the Red Cross, while in the eastern areas the Red Crescent is its counterpart.

❖

In Syria, red coloured good luck tokens are found in domestic areas and a "red-hand" token is still used in India and parts of Turkey for much the same reason. There are people who use red ink who like to think that they are adventurous. There is a need to be noticed because they are often impulsive and excitable.

Yellow is supposed to be a very unlucky colour in almost every theatre in the Western world. It should not be used for advertising material or for labels or sheet music in the orchestra pit. In other realms of activity, this is often used as a safety colour because of its high visibility and, therefore, it is a lucky colour.

❖

Yellow flowers were brought into houses in the Isle of Man to keep away the fairies. Even today there are many gardeners who will plant sunflowers in their garden corners. This is so that the fairies and little people can enjoy life in sheltered spots without having to reveal themselves.

❖

Yellow is often associated with intelligence because it has been found to stimulate the mind and has been used to decorate classrooms and some hospital wards for this purpose. Yellow is also linked with health matters as well. Some people write with yellow or gold ink and this usually reflects an inherent intuitive nature.

❖

Orange generally tends to be associated with red superstitions but one belief in particular that still exists is that a bride should carry a bouquet with at least a couple of orange flowers in it to symbolise procreation. Orange has almost always been used to encourage the growth of affection between young lovers in many Western countries.

❖

In many parts of France, violet is largely thought to be unlucky because Napoleon adopted the colour and the flower as a part of his insignia. Elsewhere, farmers dislike the colour and the flower for they believe it stops chickens from laying eggs and that baby chicks will be sickly and not grow.

In Greece, the Athenians say that Venus changed all white violets to purple because she was jealous of the love Cupid had for them. Violet is often used to help ease headaches. Those who write with this colour tend to be socialites. These folk tend to flit from one gathering to another as if they have nothing better to do. Generally, the past holds more for them than the future.

❖

Purple has always been called the colour of royalty and wealth because in those far off days it was a most expensive and rather rare colour to mix or create. It was usually reserved for a select few who could afford it. Early priests adopted purple because it was believed that it had a divine association.

❖

One very old expression to describe someone as especially lucky is "to be born to the purple", and that has been taken to mean he or she was very fortunate. However, this colour is, perhaps, viewed with a tinge of envy as in some of the very old civilisations commoners were forbidden to wear purple.

❖

Gold and silver have always had their special beliefs. Gold, because of its association with wealth has obvious connotations but it is also used in lucky charms and medical "cures". Rub a sty with a gold wedding ring nine times and the inflammation should disappear.

❖

Women about to give birth were decorated with gold to ease their confinement. In early medieval times many quack doctor-type practitioners would use instruments that looked as if they were made of gold to not only perpetuate the myth but also to impress their clientele.

In 1386 it was recorded that gold blended in a drink was a cordial and an excellent tonic for the heart. There may well have been a grain of truth in this for the word cordial has its roots in Latin from the word for heart.

❖

In the year 1665, when the great plague of London started in the July (during the passage of the Sun through Leo, which represents gold, many people would keep a piece of gold in their mouths to stop them catching the disease. False gold teeth were initially thought to have a similar effect for they were believed to help offset ill health.

❖

One of the oldest beliefs of the benefits of gold may be witnessed by fishermen all over the world who wear one gold ring in their ear. This is for two reasons. It is widely believed such a ring would prevent a seaman from drowning, while another equally ancient belief claims that this is how fishermen carry their wealth with them. It is also said that the bigger the ring, the richer the sailor.

❖

Banks and other financial organisations tend to use gold and silver with black discreetly interwoven in their decor. When used together, they can easily emphasise the necessary joint image of wealth and security.

❖

Silver is the gift of the Moon, for that is her currency. Many people who cannot abide gold turn to silver to show for their riches. Silver may be used as an alternative to gold almost everywhere except in South America and Mexico where gold has always remained the most potent of metals when it comes to superstitious beliefs. Many Cancerians tend to prefer silver to gold for this the colour of their ruling planet.

It is not widely known that the full verse for a bride to enjoy a long and happy married life reads: "something old, something new, something borrowed, something blue and a silver sixpence in your shoe". The coin should be worn in the left shoe to bring the luck. As recently as 1958, this belief was obeyed in Northern Scotland and at a wedding I attended in New Malden in Surrey. A dozen or so years later in Cambridgeshire, an old woman placed a silver sixpence on the buttocks of a new born baby, less than a minute old, slapped it and cried out for the devil to stay away.

◈

It is a common superstition that a silver bullet will destroy a werewolf or other demonic beast. You should always pass silver coins across a gypsy's before he or she reads your palm. In ancient Rome two bridesmaids would precede a bride, each holding a dish of silver coins. Just prior to a marriage a small silver coin would have been put under the main entrance to the house the happy couple intended to use to bring good luck.

◈

Many traditional May Day celebrations involve the use of silver. Milkmaids would do their hair up with silver ribbons before they could lead the dancing among the revellers. Young men would toss "heads or tails" with silver coins to see who would seek the favours of the young girls. Successful suitors would keep that coin and, if all turned out well, it might well have been the same coin put under the threshold of the house the newlyweds were to eventually live in.

◈

The origin of colour, its significance and role in superstitious belief can be traced back to the dawn of time when our ancestors still lived in caves and life was dictated by the opposing forces of night and day or the dark and the light.

◈

The dark colours have come to be associated with the passive response in our temperament, for they equate with the night, of our lowered resistance and general slowing down. The light colours that represent daylight may be said to suggest activity, incentive and energy.

It is interesting to note how sportsmen and women dress in the lighter or active colours while the more restrained or responsible types – businessmen, wear the darker colours. In the past few years or so it has become the custom for office workers especially to "dress down" on Saturdays and wear lighter colours. Of late this has also spread to the Friday.

NAMES AND NUMBERS

In many cultures it is believed to be unlucky to name a child after an aunt or an uncle, the parents, grandmother or grandfather. This is more so if that person has died recently. In the dim and distant times it was expected the youngster might suffer the same fate. These days it is more or less a condition in some families that a newly born youngster should bear at least one ancestor's name to help perpetuate the memory of that worthy person.

It is thought a 7-letter name is lucky but that 13 letters is unlucky. In parts of the west of England it was thought very unlucky to let anyone know the name of a new born child before it was actually christened, and that even included the god-parents. In recent times, it has become a custom for would-be parents to not reveal the name of their expected offspring until it has actually been born.

The myth of a "public" and "private" name is still perpetuated in the southern European and Mediterranean areas. The North American Indians also believe this. The real or private name was thought sacred and kept secret. In some of these areas, when a boy reaches puberty, the local elders will give him another name and it is expected that only he would know it and keep it concealed.

In medieval times in Middle England it was the practice when a new witch was to be initiated into the Craft that he or she should adopt a witch name which is never to be repeated outside the Circle. This tradition is still carried on in modern 21st century covens in the UK. American women use their maiden name to carry on their commercial career because it is thought unlucky for them to use their married one or that it will bring bad luck to the marriage.

This is also now being practised by some women in parts of the southern UK. Also, it seems to have become a practice nowadays for more and more newlywed couples to hyphenate their name which accounts for quite a number of "double-barrelled" couples in many parts of the UK.

The ancient Egyptians went to extraordinary lengths to stop others from learning their real names, as did the Romans for a long time because they were a very superstitious lot. The art of concealment of the name reflects a belief in the magical arts. It was thought that if others learned their real name they could inflict damage by physical injury or by spreading malicious tales in their name.

This, and variations of the practice are as widespread as Australia in the southern hemisphere to the Eskimos in the north. Some of the older people would take on a new name in the vain hope it would confuse the gods when they came to collect the soul when they died. In this way, they also thought they would gain a new lease of life because their new name was not in the Book.

Just about all superstitions regarding the name point to a belief in magic. For centuries it has been thought there was magic in the name of everything. Names are composed of letters and, in turn, the letters have a number value that are basically qualified and quantified in two different ways.

Simple numerology is the easy way. Numerology is defined as a supposed occult significance of numbers as applied to the letters of the alphabet when they make up a name. Their individual and overall values are said to have an esoteric meaning and these are used in the interpretation of the character and personality of the individual.

❖

The hard way is when these values are assessed using the Cabbala, or the Jewish mystic tradition of number. These two ideologies often give quite similar results. However, "lucky" or "unlucky" number superstitions are a completely different matter altogether.

❖

Most people have some knowledge of numerology, tone of the character assessment disciplines that can also be used to determine past and possible future events. Each letter of the alphabet is assigned a numerical value from 1 to 26. When double figures are reached, add them together then reduce to a single digit.

❖

Thus, the 13th letter of the alphabet is "m" and corresponds to 4, (1+3). For those who would like to experiment the full alphabet is set out below.

A B C D E F G H I J K L M N O P Q R S T U V W X Y Z
1 2 3 4 5 6 7 8 9 1 2 3 4 5 6 7 8 9 1 2 3 4 5 6 7 8

To arrive at the numerological value of the name you must add up all the individual values and reduce the total to a single digit.

For example:

M I C H A E L S M I T H
4 9 3 8 1 5 3 1 4 9 2 8 = 57 or 5 + 7 = 12 or 1 + 2 = 3

33 or 3 + 3 = 24 or 2 + 4 =
6 + 6 = 12 or 1 + 2 = 3

Michael Smith, therefore, is a number 3 person.

For a birth date or "fadic" number, add up the birth numbers and reduce them to a single digit as well. Michael was born on 7 July 1965, and his number is 8 (7 + 7 + 1 + 9 + 6 + 5 = 35 or 3 + 5 = 8)

Practise using your name or that of relatives and friends. It is better to use the name by which these folk are most widely known. For example, men called Richard may be known as Dick, Rick, Ricky or Rich. With the ladies, Margaret may be Maggie, Marge, Peg or Peggy.

Always check and re-check your arithmetic carefully before you read these interpretations because it is so easy to make mistakes, which will make the exercise meaningless.

NUMBER 1

These folk dislike red tape or restraint and insist on speaking their minds. They are natural leaders and individualists, not always seen to fit in to a set pattern although they can become set in their ways a little early in life. They plan well but they expect their plans to come to fruition promptly for they dislike delays. They need to exercise a lot more tolerance than they normally do.

NUMBER 2

This type prefers to work quietly in the background for they love peace and harmony. Gentle and courteous in manner, these people easily become depressed when things go wrong and there may be a lack of self-confidence. Despite this, they do have a way of working with others and are often the power behind the throne. They make good number 2's in business.

NUMBER 3

This group prefers to keep on the move, are ambitious and never really satisfied in routine work. Variety in both their leisure and business interests always attracts. They can worry themselves silly over trivia if things are not quite right. Conscientious, practical, they are good hosts with a natural charm and sense of humour.

NUMBER 4

Independent, sensitive, loyal but a little rebellious at times, these people are easily hurt by the wrong word or deed. They are conservative in their ways or mode of dress or can exhibit a rebel streak and take the opposite view. They act better as part of a team and always dream of getting away from it all but rarely do so in the end.

NUMBER 5

There can be a lack of perseverance and these people will try anything once just for the experience – twice if they like it. Versatile, quick, open and friendly, there is a wide circle of friends and acquaintances. They are changeable, restless and dualistic and hard people to reform but they are noted for their integrity.

NUMBER 6

Rather sentimental, quiet, but with a happy knack of being able to make and keep friends at all levels, for they have a natural magnetism with an equal refinement of manner. Stubborn beyond belief when they choose, they love and hate with an equal intensity. Some can appear to be hard and dislike opposition, but this is almost always a bluff.

NUMBER 7

Fond of occult matters, often rather difficult to get to know closely, their principles can be hard to understand or define. This group must have total freedom and independence at all times. Restless, they have a great love of travel. A law unto themselves, they have little time for rules and regulations but are loyal and honest friends.

NUMBER 8

These people are ruthless, hard and practical and often become perfect business machines. They are achievers and survivors for they work and play with an equal intensity. They won't hurt you or cause harm unless they themselves are threatened. Fatalistic, it is difficult for them to adapt. They prefer the tried and trusted and dislike anything new.

NUMBER 9

There is an in-built desire for leadership, perhaps more for the power that goes with it. Generally constructive, honest and solid, they are often over critical, but find it difficult to accept criticism. There is often a vigorous air about them; they cannot sit still for long. Hard to live with, they zealously preserve their freedom. There is a knack of being able to reverse disadvantage to advantage.

◈

Generally speaking, people with the same number tend to get along fairly well but there will always be a clash of personalities when two or more people who act and think alike are drawn together for any length of time.

◈

The numbers themselves have a fascination for the superstitious too and much of the blame may be laid at the door of Pythagoras, the acknowledged father of numerology and number beliefs.

He believed all numbers had a character and personality. He further maintained they were either male or female but this was meant in the sense of positive and negative. What he said and taught was recorded and even the great Plato became an ardent admirer and follower of his teachings some 200 years later.

Centuries after this, we find that, despite what individuals may believe, some civilisations and cultures actually have their favourite numbers. In the same way the English think of 7 as a lucky number, the Russians do as well. The Germans seem to have a liking for number 5 and the Chinese favour 2 and, to a lesser degree, the number 5 as well.

All the odd numbers are thought of as masculine and are largely lucky while the even numbers are regarded as feminine and relatively unlucky. But once again, it depends on where you live because in some areas even this has been changed.

❖

Number 1 is more or less universally considered as lucky, and 2 unlucky. However, in some cultures 3 and 4 are thought of as lucky and 5 and as unlucky. A survey recently suggested that the unluckiest number of all is 13, the reasons for which have been fully dealt with elsewhere.

❖

Hotels will often refuse to have a room number 13 preferring to call it 12A or 14 or, as some management authorities do, they make it the laundry room. In some of the really tall buildings, especially abroad, the 13th floor has been re-numbered also as either 12A or 14.

❖

In some central European areas, the numbers 9, 12 and 22 are considered to be very unlucky as part of the address of a house, but there are no clear-cut reasons for this.

❖

It is not just these basic numbers that are considered unlucky but also a compound version that reduces down to one is often viewed in a similar light. Thus, number 148, $(1 + 4 + 8 = 13)$ or other similar compound numbers are also a number to avoid.

❖

No. 1 symbolises the deity, whatever your belief, and 2 represents a symbol of diversity in the sense of positive and negative, of light and dark.

❖

It is viewed as very unlucky by ruling or royal dynasties all over the world, especially in France and England, because so many kings who bore the name for the second time have failed to live a full life span.

Four English kings bear witness to this, for William II was killed and it was alleged that Henry II died of grief. Later, Edward II was murdered and so was Richard II. Further on down the succession, George II died rather suddenly. It might be interesting to know how others view the present UK Queen, Elizabeth ll and the ills one might associate with her reign.

❖

In France, Charles II was poisoned. Henry II's death was predicted long before he was killed during a tournament. The long list is fascinating for those who might want to pursue this line of investigation.

❖

Number 3 symbolises the Holy Trinity in many religions and in both the old and the new. It has a strong role in Freemasonry ritual and has always been considered as a lucky number. In astrology, it is said the third day after the New Moon is regarded as very lucky.

❖

Number 4 is associated with the elements, fire, earth, air and water. It represents practicality and is frequently linked with the number 1 in esoteric studies. It features very strongly in Chinese, Indian and Mexican superstitions.

❖

Number 5 has lucky connotations with good luck, especially in the old Greek and Roman times when amulets featuring this number were worn by them to ward off the evil spirits. The pentacle or 5-pointed star has always been used in magic and ritual as a defence talisman.

❖

Number 6 is usually lucky and is often regarded as a perfect number, for it is the sum of its constituent parts $(1 + 2 + 3 = 6)$ and was sacred to the Goddess Venus thus encouraging its use for sex, love and romance when forecasting or predicting future events. In esoteric studies, the number corresponds to the choice between good and bad.

Number 7 is sacred, mysterious, fortuitous and used in a wide variety of different ways to promote good luck. The 7th day after the New Moon was set aside for sacrifices; there are 7 days of the week, the 7 ages of man and 7 colours of the rainbow to name but a few associations. In history there is hardly a country that does not venerate number 7 one way or another.

❖

Number 8 has never enjoyed a popular press and is regarded as unlucky just about everywhere. As a rule, it is linked with the planet Saturn, or the balance wheel, justice and fair play when it was used as the symbol of purification by the Egyptian God Thoth when he anointed those who were to be admitted into the secrets of the priests.

❖

Number 9 has a strange history. For a long time it has been avoided as the number for a house not only in Britain but also in middle European areas. In England, the old Fleet Prison was located at number 9 Fleet Street and an address to be avoided by anyone. In Buddhism, the number 9 enjoys great veneration in old Tibet, ancient Mongolia and China.

❖

It is a curious thing but, no matter how many times you multiply it by any other number or a combination of numbers adding up to 9, the sum will always add up to 9 ($9 \times 3 + 27$, $27 \times 9 = 243$. $45 \times 72 = 3240$ and so on). When using numerology, it can be discarded or ignored when "reducing" to the single final number.

❖

And there we end this brief survey of lucky and unlucky numbers, although all numbers from 1 to 99 all have various connotations of good or bad luck associated with them accordingly. History is alive with all kinds of tales and yarns where numbers have played a special role in the life of just one man, of individuals or even whole countries.

The United States and its association with the number 13 has long been known with much of it deriving from masonic matters. As late as the middle 1930's, the United States was busy re-arranging some of its dates and associations, partly for astrological reasons but mostly with numbers firmly in mind at the time.

❖

The murderer, Doctor Crippen, was plagued by the numbers 4 and 8 as was the explorer Captain Cook.

❖

King Charles II of England, born 29 May 1630, had many adventures before and after the Restoration on the 29th day of any month.

❖

Sir Winston Churchill, throughout his long and varied life, experienced many good and bad times on 3 or 7 days and another earlier politician, W E Gladstone, seemed to be ruled by the number 5 as did King Louis XIV of France.

❖

Our present queen, Elizabeth II, hardly seems to make an important move without the number 7 appearing time and time again in her life. Because her life is so well documented it is very easy to check important events through the archives time and time again.

❖

Readers are invited to experiment and investigate their own life. They could find they have a particular lucky and/or unlucky number running throughout their life as well. For those who do take the time, remember to check the dates of important events and birthdays of people who have or still do have an influence on you as well.

The Natural World

Almost everywhere you go, especially in the countryside, the area will be replete with superstitions and beliefs regarding plant life. Whether it is a flower, fruit, a plant or a vegetable, a thought or belief will probably be associated with it.

Even the path or road on which we travel is not forgotten and nor is the method of transportation – even now in the year 2020. Most superstitions can be traced to an understandable origin of some kind, while others can completely defeat any attempts at research.

The importance of plant life cannot be denied but it isn't widely known that they gave us the first clues to setting up a working calendar from where we began to understand the sequence of the seasons.

At the start of life, everything was probably green which, for some, is a lucky or an unlucky colour because it is nature's own. We owe much of our folklore, beliefs and superstitions to all green and other coloured plant life. In many cases, it is fairly straightforward but in others, there are quite nebulous or tenuous connotations.

◈

Flowers, it is said, are the gifts of the gods. Some must never be picked or given as a gift. This doesn't help at all when someone asks for a flower because it is thought to be most unlucky to refuse the request. All flowers are said to have hidden meanings and were often used to convey messages between lovers. This practice reached its height between the middle 17th to the late 18th centuries.

◈

Young ladies, who were normally thought of as powerless to act on their own initiative, used to take almost every opportunity to let their young men know exactly what they felt and thought about them. In turn, the young bucks who really didn't fully understand such things would reply in much the same vein. The hard-line fathers and clucking mothers of those times were (apparently) completely innocent of what was going on under their very noses or, perhaps, it might better to say that they chose to be.

❖

In a book first published nearly 150 years ago there is complete list of which flowers to use to formulate questions and how to reply or what to avoid saying because of either a local belief or a wider ranging superstition. Much of the content would have been gleaned and gathered over many years prior to this small publication, giving to all and sundry a "language of love" considered by so many in those far off days as a purely private affair.

❖

At formal gatherings, many arrangements would have already been signed, sealed and settled through such a secret language of flowers long before the occasion got under way.

❖

In the USA, if a young man had sent an ivy geranium to his young lady he was asking to dance at least one quadrille with her. A small sprig of mugwort in reply would have signified her happiness. However, these messages would be hidden among other more normal floral tributes. But even the surrounding flowers or plants could have held messages to go with the main one.

❖

Peach blossom (from him to her), suggested that "your charms are quite unequalled" and, while swooning over this flowery passion she would tell of "her woman's love" for him by sending a small bunch of pink carnations.

The message, "You are worthy of all my praise and you are my divinity", involved a small sprig of fennel and cowslips bound together in a more innocent floral arrangement and greenery to offset what was really being said. Her reply might have been with a honey flower and a garden daisy that meant, "My love is sweet and tender and I share your sentiments." And so it went on. Messages could have been less passionate when an affair came to an end if or when she sent him a Michaelmas daisy meaning "Farewell!"

❖

While it could be said that the language of flowers does not strictly belong in the realms of superstition, many thought that not to answer in the same vein was extremely unlucky. In those days of yore few, if any, young ladies seemed to have wanted to remain single. This was one way of ensuring some romantic communication with a man.

❖

Many of these flowery romantic notions stemmed from the beliefs in the efficacy of plant life in medicinal matters. It was widely believed that when a plant was not to have been used in healing then it probably played a part in religious beliefs and practices.

❖

Like holly, for example. It has always featured positively in belief and superstition. Before we came to use it for decorations at Christmas time, the old Celtic Pagans brought it indoors to help protect the house from witches and wizards.

❖

Once the established Church became aware of the practice, it soon followed that this was not a respectable pursuit and the idea and practice soon tailed off, yet despite the pressure from the Church, holly is still used today in Christmas decorations.

Its evergreen leaf has long been viewed as a symbol of eternal life and since the berries were alleged to have turned red and the leaves became prickly after the Crucifixion, it has always been held in high regard. There are those who claim that the crown of thorns was made from holly, after which the berries turned red with shame.

❖

Even away from Christian celebrations, holly holds charm status for many country folk who keep a berried sprig in the kitchen and the nursery. If it is brought indoors by a man, it should be male holly. If by a woman, it must be female. Male holly is of the prickly variety while the female type has smooth leaves. Either way, it has always been very unlucky to step on a holly berry of either sex.

❖

When the celebrations are over, holly must never be burned but allowed to degrade in the usual way. The twigs should not be broken or stamped on to help dispose of them. It is also thought best to return the waste and replace them under the tree from which they were originally taken. If this tree is in the house grounds then there will be good luck all that year which will be enhanced if this tribute is fulfilled on or before the twelfth night.

❖

A small infusion of the holly leaf sprinkled on the heads of new born babies preferably after they have been baptised will keep away evil spirits. In many farming areas, whip handles are made of holly wood to offset horses falling ill or being worried by fairies or sprites.

❖

Culpeper suggested that a dozen or so berries were good for purging the system. In those days perhaps they would but not today. If they are taken internally they will cause severe stomach cramps, vomiting and diarrhoea which, when you think about it, is one way to purge the system.

The oak ranks in equal importance in belief and superstition with holly. The Druids revered it, as did the Celts and quite a few from Northern Europe. Its wood has been used for all types of building, from ships to houses and churches.

❖

In Ireland it was one of the Seven Noble Trees of Irish law along with the alder and the apple, the birch, hazel, holly and willow trees. It is still considered very unlucky to cut, trim or chop down an oak, especially if has mistletoe growing on it. It widely believed that the oak screams when felled and those who hear the sound are doomed.

❖

Oaks are also sacred to the great Norse God Thor. He will protect you so that you cannot be harmed by lightning when you shelter under it in a thunderstorm. Some folk still keep a few acorns spread along window sills and frames. This tells Thor they are protected and that the house must not be harmed.

❖

Long, long ago, the oak was known as the marriage tree. In those days and still occasionally in a few places today, a Pagan would (or does) hold his or her wedding ceremony beneath the spreading boughs of the oak tree. After the Christian Church banned the practice, it became the fashion (and belief) for newly-weds in medieval times to travel from the church to an oak tree to repeat their vows and so make the best of both worlds.

❖

I attended one such ceremony in the early 1960s near the Rollright Stones in central southern England. A few young couples also "jumped the broom-stick" on a mid-summer eve Pagan-fest. I found this to be a most fascinating ritual to observe. In Cumberland, near Brampton, there still is a marriage oak tree where, and until recently, bridal pairs have been known to dance round it three times "for luck".

Oak trees were once used to mark village boundaries and the old-style Rogation processions would stop at them for a short service to be held. This would include a reading from the Gospels. The trees used became known as Gospel Oaks. This is still commemorated by the railway station in West London called Gospel Oak.

These trees are said to be very lucky and at certain times of the year at the Full or New Moon young girls would go at midnight to pick up the fallen acorns. They would then drop two into a bowl of pure water. If the acorns stayed close together then the girl and her current beau would stay together. If they drifted apart, so would the sweethearts. Needless to say, the more impressionable would have had (and still do) several attempts at this until they got the right answer.

❖

There is an old weather lore belief that many rural folk still hold as an indication of what to expect in the coming summer months:

"If the ash is out before the oak, we will have a soak.
If the oak is out before the ash, we'll only get a splash."

❖

There are many other tree beliefs. The ash tree is revered in many rural areas for what magical powers it has are powerful. It is allegedly disliked by snakes that won't go near it. It also has rather unfortunate links with the English royal family.

❖

If the ash-keys, the seed of the ash, fail to grow, it is said the English royal family will suffer a death within the year. It is believed there was such a failure in the summer of 1648 and Charles I was beheaded in the following January of 1649. Sometime later, in 1668, when James II visited Salisbury he suffered an almost incurable nosebleed. Local help was sought and a small piece of ash was cut and applied direct to the royal nose whereupon it instantly stopped bleeding.

In Greece and the Scandinavian countries, it is sacred and magical, for it is claimed that the Norse gods made a man from this tree and a woman for his mate from the alder tree when they wanted to populate Midgard.

❖

While it has some connections with thunder and lightning similar to the oak, the ash tree is said "to court the flash" and people should not shelter under it in a storm. It was fairly rare for one to be cut down and used for buildings because it was thought to be dangerous in the circumstances. It is still used in cures and often figures in divination and lucky charms. In Scotland, shepherds would use a crook made of ash to protect sheep from werewolves and other evil creatures of the night.

❖

Some country folk still try to find a suitable ash tree of no older than three or four years and cut small twigs precisely when the Sun enters Taurus. These were cut up and sold as good luck charms.

❖

One cure for a child's bed-wetting problem was to send him or her to collect as many leaves as they could carry in one arm. They were burned in the hearth while the child urinated on them. After this, it was alleged that they were cured.

❖

To command good luck, one wore or carried a certain amount of ash leaves. To be especially efficacious it had to be an even-ash, that is, with even divisions on both sides – a very rare occurrence.

❖

As long ago as the 1st century AD it was observed that snakes avoided ash trees. In 1785 an adder was seen to chase a small child. As he ran, the youngster passed into the shade of an ash but the snake stopped instantly. It stayed for a few moments but would not follow and eventually turned and went back the way it had come.

The evergreen yew tree has had a chequered history in respect of good and bad luck through the years. It is reputed to be a symbol of immortality and very unlucky to break or cut a branch, as they were often found growing in a churchyard or used in building churches. Whoever did so would suffer twelve months bad luck or even death before the year was out.

◈

Small sprigs of yew used to be placed alongside a dead man or woman as they were laid in their coffin just before its lid was nailed down for the last time. The yew tree is a symbol of eternal life and even today a sprig is given to sick people to help prolong their life. If this fails, it was already there to help them through into the next life.

◈

It is extremely unlucky to use yew greenery in Christmas decorations but then this tree should never be brought indoors. It is acceptable to wear or carry a piece as a charm but not as an ornament. Some rural people say if you lose something and are unable to find it, break a small branch of yew at night, wait until daylight and then hold it in your left hand as you begin your search. The branch will turn in your hand as you approach the lost property.

◈

Tree worship and reverence is traced back many years when people thought that the spirits of the gods inhabited them. They would go to a tree, knock on it for permission to speak and then make their petition. Eventually, whatever the outcome, the Tree God had or had not granted his blessing for the petitioner. This is one of the origins of the expression to touch or knock on wood for good luck. This is an exercise in superstition that is still carried on all over the world to this day.

In low magic, a tree is regarded as the supreme example of the connection between earth and heaven. It grows from the earth and takes water from it to live as it reaches to the heavens. When lightning strikes it, it is a sign from the gods that the four elements of life are as one within the tree. This suggests that fire, earth, air and water merit reverence.

❖

At one stage it was a crime to cut down a tree, punishable by death. In the history of many cultures and religions such as in Chaldea, Egypt and other countries, it was associated with the Old Testament. There are still many sacred groves and orchards where people are known set up altars under some of the trees.

❖

Apart from some fringe religious cults tree worship is still carried on in present day society. Many parents plant a tree in their garden when a child is born. For as long as the tree flourishes so will the child. Without realising it, these acts perpetuate the belief in tree magic.

❖

Some bush plants have a magic all their own and one of the best known concerns the blackberry bush. It is believed that many years ago the berries were once red, but one day the devil fell to earth and had to hide.

❖

He jumped into the bramble bush and was not discovered. However, he was so badly marked and scratched he cursed the bush which immediately made the fruit turn black. This is alleged to have occurred on the old style Michaelmas Day that would have been around October 11 or a tad earlier because of several calendar changes.

❖

In many areas since then it has long been a country superstition that to harvest or eat fresh blackberries after this date invites bad health through poisoning.

There is a very old farmers custom, "burning the bush" on New Year's Day in the morning. Hawthorn "globes" made up for Christmas decorations should be burned in open fields on the first day of the New Year. This is to bring good fortune and luck through the ever-changing seasons in the New Year.

Before daybreak on New Year's morning, some farmer's wives will bake a small piece of blackthorn made into a crown. It is then taken into the fields and ceremoniously burned. The ashes are saved and scattered over the place where the last of the previous year's wheat was sown, for this was believed to help the new crop prove extra fruitful.

❖

The mulberry is said to show the last frost of winter has passed once it shows its green leaves. If such is the case then the old saying, "cast not a clout 'til May is out" probably refers to the showing of mulberry greenery or May blossom and not, as many would say, the month of May.

Alternatively, "clout" is an old word for rags or old clothing. This saying means we should not trust the weather and go without adequate protection. However, once the May is out, that is, it is flowering, the weather becomes a lot milder and so we can start to leave off our extra winter clothing.

❖

There are many vegetable superstitions that vary slightly from area to area and a lot more so from country to country. If when preparing peas you find a pod filled with nine or more peas, you should place it above the kitchen door for good luck. In Germany you should always plant peas very early on a Wednesday or a Thursday morning to ensure a good healthy crop. To hold on to that luck, place a small onion stuck with plenty of pins on the kitchen window ledge.

❖

As we are a nation of tea drinkers, this deserves inclusion. It is considered unlucky to pour tea from a tea-pot for two or more cups at any one time. Fill one cup and then put the tea-pot back on the table. Now you may pour the second one but replace the pot on the table afterwards. Then

137

do the next and so on. As the vast majority of people now use mugs and tea-bags these days, this won't affect many but there are still a few of us left who prefer to use a cup.

❖

To maintain good luck, break the eggs to put in a cake that you are making very early but keep the shells until the cake is cooked and this will make it taste better. On the subject of cooking, always make the sign of the cross on the top of any loaf to keep the devil away. This action makes the bread rise better as well but if you should cut into a loaf and find a hole it is unlucky, for it signifies a death in the family.

❖

In this day and age, Chinese food is becoming ever more popular as we progress ever onward. However, when preparing such a meal at home, never cut long noodles for any reason, for these strips are said to confer longevity especially in China. While on the subject, young ladies in China are made to eat every grain of rice on their plate or in their bowl. Superstition maintains that, for each uneaten grain, their future spouse will have the same amount of pockmarks on his face. In that country they do not throw confetti on newly-weds as we do here in the West. Instead they throw rice, for this confers family prosperity and business success on the man.

❖

We move away from the larger plants and vegetable worlds to that of the wild flowers, herbs, weeds and other life. The language of flowers referred to earlier is one facet of all the beliefs associated with them but many wild flowers also have romances of their own.

❖

The ordinary stinging nettle bunched together with some yarrow is said to keep away ghosts if travelling at night. If the lily is blended with a laurel leaf and powdered it will prevent sleeping if placed under the pillow.

If the leaves of verbena are placed in a dovecot it encourages birds to return and they become easier to handle. A single daffodil must never be taken into or out of a house or the owner will have bad luck.

❖

The following mild low magic beliefs may have the powers that are attributed to them while some of these more bizarre superstitions are offered for the reader to experiment with.

❖

Crushed leek seeds added to vinegar help it back to full strength if it has been standing for too long. Rub apples with fresh crushed mint leaves and they will stay fresher for longer when you store them. Anyone with temporary bowel problems should chew on a few fresh sorrel leaves for this is reputed to relieve the situation. A small infusion of parsley is said to help irregular or painful periods for women.

❖

These are not old wives' tales in the strictest sense of the word, for they are genuinely believed to be efficacious. If you think something will do you good, then it will – and that is half the battle. Because of this, these little folklore remedies have taken their place in superstitious belief over a long period of time.

❖

Red or white roses (but not red *and* white together) are considered to be lucky flowers, as are the poppy, clematis, daisy, lilac and the forget-me-knot. Unlucky flowers are said to be the cyclamen, the periwinkle, peony and the geranium. As a matter of interest, both of these lists are given as flowers that a man should, or should not, accordingly, send to a woman. The azalea, dahlia, hydrangea and the marigold are also not advised as gifts. Generally speaking, most yellow flowers seem to be tainted in some way but, while some are considered as not lucky, they are all believed to be an especial protection against witchcraft.

Flowers with drooping heads, like the bluebell, daffodil or snowdrop, are thought to indicate bad luck that portends sickness or death. Poultry farmers positively loathe the primrose. It is said to stop chickens from laying or successfully hatching out their broods if brought near them.

❖

Curiously, the snowdrop or the February-fair-maid is a symbol of good luck and purity while still in the ground. It is it believed they were created from falling snowflakes by a benevolent angel who sympathised with the plight of Adam and Eve when they were driven from the Garden of Eden.

❖

It was wintertime when they left, dark and cold, so she blew on some of the snowflakes and as they touched the ground they turned into beams of light to show the couple the way to safety. Since then, these flowers seem to bloom just when they are needed to show that spring is on the way.

❖

Pathways and roads are full of superstitions and beliefs, especially the crossroads, for this is where people met originally by accident and then much later by design.

❖

For almost the whole of the Middle Ages there were no roads as such in England or anywhere else for that matter. As a rule, whatever did pass for a path was little more than a cart-track. While there were a few carriages of some kind or another, they were hardly used for long journeys because they often got stuck in the mud.

❖

The origin of the term "stick-in-the-mud" originates from the servants who were employed on what few journeys were made to help move carriages out of the mud. Great personages of either sex who had to travel usually did so on horse-back almost to the end of the 15th century and even then what passed for roads that may have been there were very badly maintained.

❖

Within a town or village, roads were little better but some semblance of order and maintenance was observed. Footpads were so called because they would cover their feet so as not to be heard and if a traveller went anywhere he risked meeting one and losing all he had as well as his life.

❖

People tended to travel in pairs or groups. As time went by, inns, public houses and hostelries began to be built where these paths crossed. Soon people began to meet at these crossroads and, eventually, this is how and where villages and townships might have started and grown up. The area would also have become a thriving trading point. To help folk travel, signposts were erected – and so were gibbets.

Highwaymen, murderers and thieves were executed at these meeting places and left dangling on the gibbet as a lesson to others of the same trade and to show travellers that there was some protection available.

❖

Superstitions and strange beliefs grew from these acts. It was usual to execute felons on a Friday morning and, in spite of other reasons given for not beginning a journey on a Friday, this soon became another. It also helps to perpetuate the myth that Friday was and is considered to be an unlucky day. In the old days, strangers were rare as were identity papers which would not have been that helpful because, except in a few very rare cases, most people couldn't read them anyway.

❖

Unfortunately, even spoken language was a problem, for dialects could change within just a few miles. If thieves and vagabonds were active in the area and a stranger was seen, he might easily have been mistaken and accused of being one of the brotherhood. At such times, one just didn't travel on a Friday.

Pathways and roads around coastal towns and villages that led to the sea were not allowed to have railings or fencing put along or across them. Stiles were not permitted either and other obstructions were torn down. This is thought to be one origin of the expression, "the freedom of the road" and is not to be confused with anti-tollgate disputes inland some years earlier. The idea was to allow for the speedier launching of boats in emergencies.

In 1911 a farmer who lived by the coast did fence off his land by cutting down a few trees, using them and the branches to do this. He was taken to court and was fined heavily for this offence.

Animal Life

It is alleged that it is the Easter Hare who really lays the Easter egg and to find one was a very lucky omen, although ordinary people were not expected to be able to see the hare itself. Those who claimed that they had were considered to be most unlucky.

❖

To meet with a loaded hay-cart anywhere has always been a lucky omen because it showed that meant that there would be plenty of bread in the following weeks, so people always gave it the right of way. In a few country areas it is thought to be a very bad thing to overtake one without first being invited to do so. In many country areas in the UK and Southern Ireland it is the custom to make a wish if you meet a cart drawn by a horse.

❖

When out walking with a friend or with an animal, it is very unlucky to allow anything or anyone to come between you. People with an animal are supposed to wait on one side to allow others to pass. It is customary in many rural areas to keep your fingers crossed to help keep the peace while others pass.

❖

Should a hare (not just an ordinary rabbit) cross your path, your journey's mission will end in misfortune, for witches were thought to turn into hares when they ventured abroad. In pre-Christian times the hare was considered a sacred animal and only ever eaten by the Goddess Estre.

Whether or not you live in town or the countryside, you will see plenty of all kinds of wildlife, particularly birds. The folklore of our feathered friends has a world of its own. No matter what time of the day or year, some birds are thought to be lucky while others are not so lucky.

❖

Because birds can fly, they were thought to be a physical manifestation of the departed but divine souls and in many areas they were worshipped as gods. Their sounds and actions were closely observed by priests and fortune-tellers who, in turn, would "interpret" their actions or calls in the best way they could. This was most prevalent in ancient Greece and Rome, although even today in many areas of this part of the world there are still a few who still "believe".

❖

Divination by birds is as old as the hills and survives still in parts of Southern Europe, the Middle East, and some African and South American countries. Black or black and white birds and those that fly at night are all considered unlucky and are considered to be in league with the devil. If these creatures are heard calling in daylight hours, it presages all manner of misfortunes for those who hear them.

❖

Light coloured birds seem better favoured except for the female blackbirds that are disliked, for they are thought to be "French" or foreign birds. Many sea birds are believed by sailors to be the reincarnation of drowned shipmates.

❖

A cage-bird is alleged to have a special affinity for the family with which it lives and must be told of a death in the family otherwise it will pine away and die. Some people still tie a small black ribbon to a cage to offset anything happening to the bird.

Many exotic birds from abroad live very long lives and bond with their human owners very early on. If kept apart for very long periods, these birds will pine and die. If the owner has been hospitalised, these days it is now generally acceptable to take the bird to visit. The greeting that each will give the other is quite unmistakable and very moving to observe.

❖

I clearly recall the behaviour of my African grey parrot "Groucho" who did not see me for almost three weeks immediately after I had a heart attack. Although my wife fussed over him as much as she could at the time, neither of us were prepared for what happened when I first got home. I had to go to bed but once I was settled she brought him to see me. It still brings tears to my eyes even now when I remember how he flew down to my chest and "covered" me with his open wings making all sorts of funny noises. The affection that bird showed me on that day nearly twenty years ago and still does even now is something I shall never forget.

❖

Here in the UK, the robin has many superstitious beliefs concerning it. It is very unlucky to harm a robin, its eggs or nest. It is said that even the devil will go after anyone who desecrates the robin's world. If people break its eggs, something belonging to them will be broken; if they harm a chick, so will they be harmed.

❖

We have a wild robin in our garden that is virtually a pet. First thing in the morning he waits for one of us to go out and, as we feed all the other animal life, he gets his on a special plate in a special place that no other bird will go near while he is about. He always says thank you afterwards. Should either of us have a spade or a fork with which to dig for any purpose, he is there like a shot. We have to stop when we might turn over a juicy worm or some insect he fancies. He is great company.

To kill a robin in the countryside brings great misfortune to whoever does so. If you are really observant, you will notice that even the local cats seem to give them a wide berth. One old belief says that if a cat does manage to catch and kill one, it will itself lose a limb.

❖

The robin is said to have got his red breast in several ways. One tried to help Christ by managing to draw out one of the thorns from the crown to ease His discomfort. It was stained by the Lord's blood as it did so but was allowed to keep its now new red breast in remembrance of what it had tried to do.

❖

Another superstition suggests that a robin took pity on souls in Purgatory and tried to take water to them but was scorched badly for its pains. God allowed the bird to keep the colour as an example of its goodness. It is also said that if a robin finds a dead body, it will cover the face to prevent damage to it or it will stay by its side and sing until someone else comes along to do what has to be done.

❖

However, it does have its bad side. If a robin taps at a window, a death will occur shortly in that house. If it flies inside a house or a church while a service is under way, someone present will soon leave this world.

❖

Other birds have also been associated as harbingers of doom. Two large white birds appear and just glide through the air when the Bishop of Salisbury is said to be near the end of his life. In Chichester, a heron has been seen to perch on the cathedral roof when the bishop there is dying.

❖

When an un-baptised baby dies in France, it is said that it becomes a bird and remains one until Judgement Day. In Ireland and Australia, black or grey birds that fly at night but who never seem to settle are thought to be the souls of those who lived an evil life and that their current life is their penance. A bird appearing to fly from either end of a rainbow will bring good luck if it lands near you or drops a feather as it goes by. It is said in various places in Brazil that if you pick it up and keep it safe you will never be poor.

❖

Canaries are lovely singing birds and are known for their fidelity to a mate once they have bonded. If one is quiet for too long, it is always a good thing to investigate why as they are very sensitive to atmosphere and can be moody little characters. They used to be taken down a coal mine to test the air in case escaping gas could not be detected by the miners.

❖

There is an old superstition that canaries will turn blue with a change of diet and thus become extremely valuable. This is not true, for the nearest colour to this will be a shade of grey. The only "blue canary" is the nightclub of fiction.

❖

The common sparrow cannot walk, it can only hop. This belief comes from Korea where it is said that many centuries ago a sparrow had a disagreement with a fly and they could not resolve the problem. They took the matter to a wise old man who told them both off and beat them with a whip.

❖

As he did so, the sparrow hopped up and down with the pain and the fly was hardly able to stand upright. He relented eventually but told them both they would be punished. The bird would never walk again; it would have to hop everywhere as a punishment. He also warned that whenever the fly landed in future, it had to stop and rub its feet together in memory of the pain brought on through a silly dispute.

The ladybird or ladybug with its scarlet coat and black spots is very popular with youngsters and is associated with good luck provided one lands on you. You should blow it off, not nudge it away. Each spot is supposed to indicate its age and if one with seven spots lands upon you, it extremely fortunate. Curiously, most ladybirds only usually live for about year, as a rule.

❖

When one lands on the hand of girl engaged to be married and crawls all over it, it is said to be measuring for her wedding gloves. If the girl was not going to wear gloves, she had to do so now or it would bring bad luck. Curiously, this belief is also said of grasshoppers in some European countries.

❖

The busy bee, long revered by country folk for many reasons, has a fair wealth of stories. Never try to brush one away from you or off you if it lands. Talk to it quietly and ask it to go home. You should do the same if one comes into a house or a car. Allow it to crawl on your hand and let it fly away safely. It is very unlucky to kill a bee. It is widely believed that bees have to be told in advance of a wedding or a funeral. A small piece of white ribbon for a wedding or black for a funeral should be fixed to the hive as you tell them. It is thought that if this is not done, they will swarm. It is unlucky to buy or sell bees, one should try to obtain them through barter. In some countries, they could be paid for in gold coin but there is now no such currency. In Northern England it is said that when bees fail to produce honey, there will be serious local troubles. On the European continent, in America and the Middle East some claim it is thought to portend war.

❖

Ordinary everyday beetles are largely unlucky unless one crawls into an empty shoe which is thought to imply monetary luck. If you wear the shoes and then find the creature dead or alive (?) it suggests a death in the family is likely.

Spiders are universally disliked by just about everybody, except for those who keep them or have made a study of them. They are such beautiful little creatures. Almost all of them are very clever. extremely resourceful and gifted with the patience of a saint.

❖

"If you wish to stay alive then let a spider thrive" is an old saw in many country communities. If there is no other first aid help possible, a spider's web placed across an open wound is a first class way to stem the blood flow and keep it clean. Many moons ago I did this when I suffered an accidental cut miles from anywhere. It worked wonders and did the trick beautifully. Spiders in a house are said to always be a good sign. If one should fall on you, money luck is on the way. In other lands, quite a few spiders have a poisonous bite, however large or small they may be. With the exception of the well-known deadly black widow, the tarantula and a few others, they rarely cause serious problems. They almost never attack but if they do, it is because they have been threatened.

❖

The harvest spider or daddy-longlegs is very lucky and never does harm. If one is in the way, pick it up and put it somewhere safe outside the house. As there are nearly forty thousand varieties of spider, one can understand that it might be better to spare just one if it strays.

❖

Fish are reputed to have great wisdom and those that live in wishing wells or healing spas are alleged to embody the souls of great people who have decided to stay and help heal the sick. Of course, these fish are regarded as sacred and are allowed to live undisturbed.

❖

It is believed in France that fishing is poor off the Normandy coast because they left when the royal family was deposed. But locals always believed that if the crown were to be restored, the fish would return.

When the season starts, fishermen anxiously examine the first fish caught, for this determines the success or failure of the period. If it is a female, it marks an excellent time ahead but a male suggests a thin time of it. To ensure a good catch, the first fish caught is nailed to the mast but if someone counts the fish as they are caught, that haul will be poor.

❖

Superstition has it that fish should be eaten from the tail to the head and never the other way. It is claimed that there is less likelihood of a bone being caught in the throat, a story that is completely untrue. After the meal, it is unlucky to burn the fish bones, instead bury them and allow them to decompose naturally.

❖

In olden times and in many areas, fishermen would sacrifice the first fish they caught to Poseidon the ancient God of the Sea. This was to appease the god, for men would eat fish to draw off the strong fertility powers associated with the denizens of the deep.

❖

Because of their acknowledged fecundity, fish were dedicated to Venus and the Christians dedicated them to the Virgin Mary and at the same time decreed that fish were to be eaten only on a Friday, once known as Virgin Day or Fish Day. It was thought to be a mortal sin to eat meat of any kind on a Friday and extremely unlucky. Until fairly recently, fish used to be the main alternative offered at school lunch times.

❖

Oysters have their place in the realms of superstition. It has always been thought wrong to eat oysters if there is not an "R" in the month in the belief that they were poisonous at such times. This idea, along with the belief that ice cream must not be eaten at the same as oysters are served in a meal, is a complete fallacy. It is alleged to be very lucky to eat oysters on the first day they appear, as did the Romans. The idea spread throughout Europe and eventually found its way to the USA. It is now an established tradition to send oysters to the White House at the start of its season.

In parts of America, some people think that oysters grow on trees and in essence this is partly correct. Oysters are known to attach themselves to mangrove trees whose roots often extend into the sea and, therefore, some of them do actually "grow on trees".

❖

In the animal kingdom, the cat reigns supreme when it comes to strange beliefs and superstitions and no animal has had more written about it than the cat. Many cat-cults worshipped felines in Egypt. They held them in very high esteem although it was thoroughly disliked throughout almost all of the Middle Ages and beyond because of its association with witchcraft and, even today, they are either thought of as a harbinger of misfortune or a symbol of good luck.

❖

The Egyptian cat-headed god, Bast, revered all feline life. When cats died, the owners and family would go into full mourning, along with supplying the most expensive funeral rites in its memory. Cats everywhere have always been thought a symbol of mystic powers for good or ill. Worshippers of Diana in Roman times, and later Freya in Norse legends, revered all cats, who were placed under their special protection. In particular, Freya's chariot was drawn by cats.

❖

As a result of these many different beliefs and superstitions, cats are either lucky or unlucky, dependent on where you live. Generally speaking, in England, black cats are generally considered to be unlucky, while in some areas white cats are thought to be even more unlucky.

❖

In America, Spain, Italy and other southern European countries, the black cat is unlucky, while the white cat is thought to be lucky. However, white cats are not normally that popular because they are often deaf. The tortoise-shell is widely believed to be lucky in Britain but unlucky in France.

The blue cat is considered very favourably in Russia and satellite areas but unlucky elsewhere. In these countries, a cat was often made to lie in a cradle before a new-born baby used it, so that it would have good luck.

❖

The writer, Edgar Allan Poe, did nothing to help the cause of the cat when he wrote some of his stories that perpetuated the many cat myths. When a cat enters a house or boards a ship of its own accord it is thought to be very lucky, especially if it stays. In the old Cornwall mining areas the word "cat" was never spoken while miners were underground. When a cat left a house in which there was sickness and did not return, the sick person was expected to die.

❖

Cats will not stay in a house in which there is an unburied corpse. If one leaps across an open coffin, the soul of the lately departed will not rest in peace unless the animal is put down. May-born cats are unlucky and in many English rural areas kittens born during this month may well be killed or thrown out of the house.

❖

When cats suddenly rush hither and thither, chase their tails or bits of fluff and claw at the furniture, stormy winds are on the way. When they wash their ears all the time it means heavy rain can be expected. You should never buy a cat if you want to keep it – or it wants to stay! It is better to exchange it for something else or accept it as a gift. Cats are rather special and very affectionate – and you can't buy that.

❖

The wolf is another animal that has been much maligned and misunderstood over the years. Stories of its alleged occult abilities have built up a reputation that is ill-deserved. This affectionate and loyal beast is a great family type. It travels in packs because that is its nature but a few are literally "lone-wolves" by choice.

That a wolf is often a vampire stems from fiction and old wives' tales. Were-wolves are an invention of man. In central European areas, wolves were often seen to feed on the fallen dead after a battle and this gave rise the fables of them being demons. It is widely believed that the magpie is only tolerated in these areas as it is the only living creature that knows how to warn of the approach of a wolf.

❖

Greek gods and goddesses were believed to assume the shape of a wolf when they wanted to travel among men and years ago in Athens people had to pay to bury a dead wolf killed within the city walls.

❖

Other animals linked to witchcraft were foxes and toads. Where wolves obviously did not live, foxes became substitutes. Many is the tale of a fox being chased by hounds to a lonely cottage, only to find a little old lady sitting peacefully at her fireside when the huntsmen arrived.

❖

In Japan, there is a Fox Goddess who can take on the appearance of a wolf-temptress. When it is too late, she turns into a vixen that will kill the unsuspecting victims to help perpetuate her magical skills with his or her blood.

❖

In Wales, several foxes seen together are believed to be very unlucky, for they are normally on their own or with their partner. Today and often well within town limits, foxes are seen out and about as bold as brass foraging for food or sunbathing on a warm day. I have often seen them in Central London in Clapham Junction playing in the railway cuttings.

❖

We have almost tame foxes that regularly come for food and wait patiently for us to do just that. For quite some time, one female visitor in particular would actually take the food from my hand. In return she would bring her young to show us how many she had to feed. Just to see them gambolling across the lawn has long been sufficient reward.

Toads have little joy in superstition. To meet one is lucky in daylight hours but at night it may really be a witch on her way to perform her nefarious deeds and, therefore, quite unlucky.

❖

They are quite harmless but very helpful in the garden because they are likely to consume some of the more undesirable pests we cannot always find or destroy. A few toads have been kissed in the vain hope that at least one really was a handsome prince imprisoned in its body by a wicked fairy.

❖

Unlike other creatures, the toad is associated not only with witchcraft but also black magic. They are greatly feared in many parts of Central and Southern Europe where such practices were generally thought to be carried on.

❖

The toad was alleged to be used as a lookout hidden in the bushes where no one could see it. They would croak a warning for the ceremony to stop and as people approached deliberately put themselves in their path so it would be thought they were innocent and tame, but this was a ploy to give the witches a chance to get away.

Miscellaneous

There are an extremely wide number of superstitions not included in any of the foregoing because they do not really fall into any specific categories.

THE CROSS

For example, it is time the continual references to the "cross" were dealt with more fully with a detailed explanation. Very few people realise how many thoughts and ideas there are about their origin or their associated beliefs.

❖

There are some sixty or more different types of cross, apart from the different or "dressed" versions dedicated to individual saints, each with their own special meaning or representation. The cross is universal, an emblem of occult and sacred mysteries that was venerated for centuries even before the Christian era. Crosses of one kind or another have been found among the remains of some of the oldest known cultures now known to modern man.

❖

For example, when the Spanish first arrived in Mexico, it came as a total and quite unexpected surprise to find the natives held the cross as one of their most sacred symbols yet they had never heard of Christianity. For them, the cross was the sign of their God of Rain.

Crosses with a religious significance are all shapes. One of the oldest among them is the swastika which is one the oldest talismans of them all. It should not be viewed as the symbol of last century's Nazi Germany but as the sign of eternity encompassing the cross, the emblem of faith.

❖

All crosses are found in some way or another as a talisman or a mascot. It may be carried or worn as a decoration to fend off bad luck. For many centuries, it was seen as a symbol of sacrifice. The Assyrians, Egyptians, Persians, Phoenicians, Scandinavians and the Indians were just a few of the oldest cultures in the world to have used it. However, it is the Latin or Christian cross that most people are familiar with and it is heavily involved in all manner of belief and superstitions.

❖

To make the sign of the cross automatically summons up a basic belief in the Christian religion and the memory of Jesus Christ sacrificed on the Cross. It is also a defence gesture used against the devil and his minions because, apart from anything else, it is also the universal symbol of good luck.

❖

We cross our fingers for good luck in an act that we bring into adulthood from our childhood days. It is a reminder of when as a child we would blatantly tell the world untruths of varying natures but with fingers crossed to insure against being found out.

❖

As a charm against all manner of minor ills, the sign of the cross would be and still is made in conjunction with whatever problem besets us. A cramp would require the sign of the cross on the shoe or on the floor so the foot could be placed upon it. As a cure for hiccups, one should wet the forefinger with your tongue and draw it across the throat.

For pins and needles, the same idea is employed, except that the sign of the cross is made on the afflicted part of the body. In the middle of the 16th century a statute was issued to prevent bakers marking their bread with the sign of the cross because if any ordinary loaves were to be used in religious ceremonies they had to be unleavened, round and not otherwise marked.

❖

To offset any private belief, the baker or the housewife would make the sign of the cross in the dough as they prepared it, knowing that it would not visibly bake out. The hot-cross bun which has always been heavily symbolic of Easter and, along with that special aroma, is a familiar sight in bakers' shops in the run-up to the festival.

❖

To help preserve cheese, the sign of the cross was often scratched along the top. Eggs were marked with the sign of the cross for two reasons, to produce healthy chickens or, if they were stored to be eaten, to help preserve them until they were consumed.

❖

Gamblers sit with their legs crossed for good luck, schoolchildren sit with their legs crossed to help them through exams and women would sit cross-legged to bring their companions good luck at whatever they were doing at the time.

❖

Crosses are often placed above doors, windows or fireplaces to keep out the devil. Mince pies often have the cross etched along their tops and many farmers' wives still put the symbol on their preserves to protect them during storage.

❖

The Greek and Maltese Crosses are well known and instantly recognisable for their use in heraldry. They have been associated with many religious and superstitious beliefs for centuries. In the heraldry of the English royal regalia, both of these religious symbols are to be found. As well as these, there are also many other symbols.

The St George Cross, the symbol of chivalry or the Celtic Cross has long been an emblem of Pagan belief. The St Andrew's Cross is recognised all over the world instantly as Scotland's own. The Tau Cross is the symbol of life in many Mediterranean areas and is still worn by Greek bishops. It was also once used by the ancient Romans and the Jews in their ceremonies. It is still the symbol by which the Franciscan Order of Friars throughout Europe is known.

The Wheel Cross as used by the Druids and often seen built into the side of houses in Northern Europe as a protection against evil and was prevalent for hundreds of years. It was so revered that it was actually used on the coinage of King Edward the Elder a hundred years before the Norman invasion.

As late as the 19th century, the Cross of Death was still marked outside the house of a recently departed soul when his or her demise took place outside or away from the home. This was done in order to appease or pacify the gods and to keep away the evil ones to prevent them from haunting the area.

In all probability, the marks were made to stop souls from wandering, for the crosses were often renewed on the anniversary of the death. It was not thought proper for them to become obliterated – they had to be seen at all times.

Some modern observers feel this belief may be perpetuated with the way people now place small bouquets of flowers at the scene after a death or murder. Others feel it is done to warn the living that they should avoid the place in case of a repetition and to help ward off the bad luck.

It was only in the last decade of the previous century that the most public dramatic demonstration of this was in the absolute oceans of flowers left outside the former home of the Princess of Wales after her tragic death. And quite recently a murder by gypsies of a gypsy in Surrey witnessed a similar ritual but there was no sign of the Death Cross.

PRECIOUS STONES

Precious stones along with gold and silver have their legends, beliefs and superstitions that are thousands of years old. These are not just superstitious beliefs in the ordinary sense, for in many cases they have associations with medical and religious matters.

❖

The diamond is perhaps the most precious of stones, especially where women are concerned and holds the prime position. Perhaps the widest known belief comes to mind in the expression: "diamonds are a girl's best friend".

❖

As a power against evil, the diamond has little equal. In some religious beliefs it is expected that new born babies should have a little diamond dust sprinkled on them to protect them from evil and to ensure that they will never want for material possessions.

❖

Many believe a diamond should always be worn on the left side of their body and touching the skin. This is one reason for the modern habit in the UK of wearing a diamond ring on the left hand in a clear setting. This belief is thought to help fend of those who cheat and endow the owner with a righteous outlook. It is supposed to make him fair-minded and just to his enemies as well as his friends and allies.

Diamonds are believed to have as many good portents as bad ones. It is only a favourable mascot or talisman when obtained through honest toil. When gained through a crime, the diamond can carry a terrible curse, often one that can last forever.

❖

The Koh-I-Noor Diamond is credited with a dreadful history of murder and bloodshed until it was presented to Queen Victoria in the 19th century. The Hindus stipulated it would keep its powers for good only while a man did not directly own it. In her will, Victoria ordered that it was to be passed only to a female consort or the next in line, if a woman.

❖

The Hope Diamond is almost as bad, for it has brought bad luck to all those who have owned it. The Duchess of Montespan, who had been a lover of Louis XIV of France, had no sooner received it than everything went wrong for her and she just faded out of the picture. A later owner, Marie Antoinette, was executed on the guillotine and it passed to a Dutch dealer who was robbed by his own son and eventually died in poverty and the son committed suicide.

❖

The stone then passed to the Hope family who were plagued by misfortune at almost every step until it was sold in the early 1900's to a Middle Eastern potentate who later lost his throne. It is thought that it went down on the Titanic along with that purchaser.

❖

One superstition long held from the Middle East was that a woman should never use a diamond as a button, for this could cause a violent end to the wearer. It has been said that when Tsar Nicholas and his family were executed, they afterwards found that each of the royal princesses were wearing buttons on their dresses made of diamonds but covered in material to hide what they really were.

The emerald has had a chequered history. Favoured by expectant mothers near their time, it was worn to protect against loss of memory and sight. In some Far East areas it is said that a snake would be struck blind if it were to attack anyone wearing an emerald.

❖

A favourite gem of Isis, the ancient Moon Goddess, it is often worn by sailors and fishermen as a protection against the threat of death at sea or shipwreck. In the East, it is often strapped to the arm of travellers to preserve them from attack.

❖

It has always been thought a special gift between lovers to ensure truth and fidelity. A ring made of pure emerald was believed to be a cure for epilepsy and dysentery. An emerald worn under the left arm will prevent other people from putting a spell on the wearer.

❖

The sapphire has many religious connotations. In the 12th century, Pope Innocent III ordained that the bishops' rings should be of gold and set with sapphires. Solomon's ring was set with a sapphire to show his great wisdom and judgement and the Jews revered the sapphire as sacred. In the East, the Buddhists maintain that one can reach a very high state when wearing the sapphire because it elevates thoughts and devotion.

❖

On a more mundane level, it is claimed that the sapphire will only keep its pure colour for as long as whoever wears it is honest, faithful and true. Royalty are associated with this particular gem for it was widely thought by many of them to preserve them from envy. It was thought to help protect them to be free from being overthrown. On the continent, some felt the sapphire prevented them from being poisoned.

Curiously, almost the same powers are thought to reside in the ruby. It should be worn to prevent quarrels between relatives and helps to guard against death by drowning. In the Middle East it is believed that if you wear one next to your skin for long enough it will change colour at the first sign of impending trouble. The ruby is mentioned in many religious writings in the East and there is a belief that it can help to control the passions when a clear mind is needed.

The pearl has several origins according to which legend you believe. The most romantic concerns Baldur, the Norse God of Light, who was killed by an arrow of mistletoe. His mother, Freya, brought him back to life with her tears. It is said her tears congealed on him and in memory of her great love, they became the pearls of the mistletoe plant.

Many Eastern countries credit pearls with a few quite varied life-giving properties. In India, they believe that powdered pearl will cure haemorrhages. It is also supposed to help prevent lunacy and mental problems from developing. To bathe in water that has powdered pearl in it helps keep the skin clean and pure. The pearl has long been associated with the Mother Goddess, the giver of life.

THE MOON

The Moon probably has more superstitions and beliefs associated with good or bad luck than anything else. A New, Full or Quarter Moon has a whole wealth of stories that are believed even to the present day. Many people from all walks of life are known to refuse to start, contact or finish all manner of tasks and projects if the Moon is in the wrong phase or sign of the zodiac. Curiously, and outside of astrology, one rarely hears of the void-of-course moon and what one should or should not do when it occurs.

There are few superstitions that refer to eclipses of which there are usually at least four each year. However, in some years, like 1969 and 1980, for example there were no lunar eclipses at all unlike solar eclipses, when there must be at least two each year.

❖

We know that eclipses have been recorded since before the 8th century BC and there is a copy of one of these lists inscribed on stone in the British Museum that was taken from Nineveh. It lists not only the kings of that period but also the eclipses that occurred during the reign. An eclipse can only occur at the time of a New or Full Moon.

❖

Each month a complete lunar cycle begins with a New Moon, followed about seven days later by the first quarter. Roughly seven days afterward, the Full Moon occurs and this, in turn, is followed about seven days or so later with the last quarter. The whole cycle is continuous and never ending.

❖

Each of the Moon's quarters has its own meanings but it is generally agreed that the New Moon is the most important for it means new beginnings. We project ourselves in a more forceful manner, people notice us as we do so. This is when we should start things and be more innovative.

❖

At the second quarter, what was started begins to take shape, so we must nurture and develop these ideas to ensure their success. At the Full of the Moon, the third quarter, such tasks should come to fruition. At the fourth quarter, it is a time for reflection and planning, to be ready to start the next task at the next New Moon.

Moon worshipping survives from many ancient cults and is still carried on today. Most were, or are, negative, sinister or evil and frequently connected with devil-worship as well. From these beliefs comes superstition, much of which is completely misunderstood by those who are not aware of the forces of nature.

❖

One should never point to the Moon or misfortune will follow. When the New Moon is seen through glass, one should bow to it, especially if it is the first moon of the year. Traditionalists should note that means the New Moon which occurs on or after March 21, for this was when the New Year used to start. These days, however, this thinking has passed to the Neomenia, which is now the first New Moon, actually a few days before, on or just after January 1.

❖

In Celtic areas, men would doff their hat and bow three times while the ladies would give a most reverential curtsey, while at the same time a version of this old rhyme was spoken, "I see the Moon, the Moon sees me. God bless the Moon, and God bless me".

❖

For good luck, all coinage must be turned over in the light of the New Moon. It is very unlucky to view any Mew Moon through the branches of a yew or willow tree.

❖

Even in these modern days, it is extremely rare for farm animals to be castrated or killed when the Moon is on the wane. Anything cut to grow at such a time is said to not do so successfully, which is why some shepherds refuse to dock lamb's tails in the dark of the Moon.

A child born in the waning of the Moon was expected to be sickly and not very strong. If a child developed whooping cough, it was taken out in the moonlight to look at the New Moon to help ease the illness.

❖

It has long been believed that when the Harvest Moon rides very high in the sky, bread prices would increase. A Full Moon on Christmas Day portends a poor harvest. The New Moon falling on a Friday, Saturday or a Sunday is called the farmer's curse (or the sailor's curse) and was also thought to adversely affect the weather.

❖

Astrologers claim that people born during these moon quarters all tend to exhibit clear-cut character and personality differences. These days, most of us are familiar with the character and personality of those who are born when the Moon passes through the twelve signs of the zodiac, in much the same way as when the Sun travels through them.

❖

Today, doctors will not perform operations at certain times of the Moon because the blood flow is said to be too high or too low or cause excess pain and suffering to the patient.

❖

Around twenty per cent of our modern calendar is determined by the time of the New Moon. The Chinese start their New Year at the second New Moon after the winter solstice of the previous year.

❖

The following moon table tells us what we may expect from life according to how many days after the New Moon we are born. If the New Moon occurs before noon, then that day is the first day. If it happens after noon, then the first day is the next day.

A New Moon falling at 10.00 hours on a Monday makes that day the first day. If the New Moon occurs at 18.00 hours on a Monday, then Tuesday is the first day.

1st day	Long-lived and fortunate.
2nd day	Good at detection.
3rd day	People of influence help out a lot.
4th day	Tendency to poor health.
5th day	Loses interest quickly.
6th day	Easily influenced.
7th day	Strong and often long-lived.
8th day	Will succeed only by their own efforts.
9th day	Generally fortunate, recognised for their efforts.
10th day	A nomad, few roots.
11th day	Open personality, a good counsellor.
12th day	The astrologer's day, a prophetic type.
13th day	Clever, perceptive and intuitive.
14th day	Uses people.
15th day	Poor health or a weak constitution.
16th day	Would make a good merchant.
17th day	Rash, unable to "read" people.
18th day	Brave and hardworking.
19th day	Will be influential but may misuse power.
20th day	Easily influenced.
21st day	Selfish and possessive.
22nd day	Popular socially, many friends.
23rd day	Long distance travel indicated.
24th day	Clever and resourceful.
25th day	Adventurous and determined.
26th day	Financially successful.
27th day	Intuitive, friendly and sociable.
28th day	Weak constitution, good family life.
29th day	Good marriage and successful career.
30th day	Scientifically orientated, happy life.

Throughout many primitive cultures, the Moon has always been a source of magic and superstition. In today's far more rational world, she is perceived with much more clarity than previously. This is because time and far more study than ever before is slowly beginning to help to yield up her secrets. This is supposed to help to make the world a better place in which to live, from a superstitious point of view, of course.

Touch wood.

Lightning Source UK Ltd.
Milton Keynes UK
UKHW022018200221
378988UK00005B/70